BrightRED Study Guide

CfE ADVANCED Higher

BIOLOGY

David Lloyd and Geoff Morgan

First published in 2016 by:
Bright Red Publishing Ltd
1 Torphichen Street
Edinburgh
EH3 8HX

Reprinted with corrections in 2017
New edition published in 2019

A CIP record for this book is available from the British Library

ISBN 978-1-84948-335-3

With thanks to:
Dr Neil Marshall, for his extensive contribution to the Investigative Biology chapter,
Leah McDowell, ELEM design, and Owen Rixon, The 2D Workshop (Illustrations),
PDQ Digital Media Solutions Ltd (layout) and Dr Anna Clark (edit)

Cover design and series book design by Caleb Rutherford – e i d e t i c

Acknowledgements
Every effort has been made to seek all copyright holders. If any have been overlooked, then Bright Red Publishing will be delighted to make the necessary arrangements.

Permission has been sought from all relevant copyright holders and Bright Red Publishing are grateful for the use of the following:

Acknowledgements
Permission has been sought from all relevant copyright holders and Bright Red Publishing are grateful for the use of the following:
Geoff Morgan & David Lloyd (p 9); Two images © David Lloyd (p 9); Image © Mystrica Ltd. (p 11); Friedrich Fröbel (CC BY-SA 3.0)[1] (p 12); piemmea (CC BY-SA 3.0)[1] (p 13); Genome Biol. 2008; 9(5): R91 (CC BY 2.0)[2] (p 13); TimVickers (CC BY-SA 3.0)[1] (p 15); Lothar Schermelleh (CC BY-SA 3.0)[1] (p 15); Karel Schmeidberger (CC BY-SA-3.0)[1] (p 17); Grzegorz Polak (CC BY-SA-3.0)[1] (p 17); Vossman (CC BY-SA 3.0)[1] (p 25); Kelvinsong (CC BY-SA 3.0)[1] (p 42); Cytoskeleton of Rat2-sm9 cells © University of Basel, imaged by R. Suetterlin, courtesy of C-A. Schoenenberger (p 42); Lordjuppiter (CC BY-SA 3.0)[1] (p 43); The Center for Cell Dynamics, University of Washington (p 45); Two images © Geoff Morgan (p 48); David Goodsell (CC BY 3.0)[3] (p 49); Egelberg (CC BY-SA 3.0)[1] (p 49); Geoff Morgan (p 50); Fourteen images © Geoff Morgan (pp 51–54); Chapman, Frank M. (CC BY 2.0)[2] (p 55); Guide to the coastal marine fishes of California in STATE OF CALIFORNIA, THE RESOURCES AGENCY, DEPARTMENT OF FISH AND GAME, FISH BULLETIN 157 by Miller, Daniel J., creator, Lea, Robert N. (1972). Courtesy of Scripps Institution of Oceanography (p 55); Two images © Geoff Morgan (p 56); Zeynep F. Altun, Editor of www.wormatlas.org (CC BY-SA 2.5)[4] (p 57); André Karwath aka Aka (CC BY-SA 2.5)[4] (p 57); Adam Amsterdam (CC BY 2.5)[8] (p 57); Three images © Geoff Morgan (p 58); Oliver Herold (CC BY 3.0)[3] (p 59); Katja Schulz (CC BY 2.0)[2] (p 59); liz west (CC BY 2.0)[2] (p 59); S. Rae (CC BY 2.0)[2] (p 59); SoulRiser (CC BY-SA 2.0)[5] (p 59); prilfish (CC BY 2.0)[2] (p 59); Rushen (CC BY-SA 2.0)[5] (p 59); CSIRO (CC BY 3.0)[3] (p 59); prilfish (CC BY 2.0)[2] (p 59); Yankech gary (CC BY-ND 2.0)[6] (p 59); Nine images © Geoff Morgan (pp 61, 62, 63 & 66); André Karwath aka Aka (CC BY-SA 2.5)[4] (p 67); Two images © Geoff Morgan (p 67); Mark Medcalf (CC BY 2.0)[2] (p 69); Three images © Geoff Morgan (p 71); Miroslav Duchacek (CC BY-SA 3.0)[1] (p 72); Image licensed by Ingram Image (p 73); Drc406 (CC BY-SA 3.0)[1] (p 73); Paul Asman and Jill Lenoble (CC BY 2.0)[2] (p 73); Image taken from Bolzer et al., (2005) 'Three-Dimensional Maps of All Chromosomes in Human Male Fibroblast Nuclei and Prometaphase Rosettes.' *Public Library of Science Journal: Biology* 3(5): e157 DOI: 10.1371/journal.pbio.0030157, Figure 7a © Public Libra (p 78); Sbharris (CC BY-SA 3.0)[1] (p 79); Geoff Morgan (p 80); Four images © Geoff Morgan (pp 80–81); Otis Historical Archives of "National Museum of Health & Medicine" (CC BY 2.0)[2] (p 82); Three images © Geoff Morgan (pp 83 & 88); The poster 'Malaria Kills A Child Every 45 Seconds' reproduced by permission of Christian Aid (p 93); The poster 'Her Love Can't Make Dirty Water Clean' reproduced by permission of Oxfam (p 93); Logo © BioMed Central/The primary paper 'In vivo genome-wide profiling reveals a tissue-specific role for 5-formylcytosine' by Iurlaro M., McInroy G.R., Burgess H.E., Dean W., Raiber E.A., Bachman M., Beraldi D., Balasubramanian S., Reik W. taken from taken from Genome Biology 2016 17:141 (CC BY 4.0)[7] (p 96); Logo © International Journal of Molecular Sciences/Review article 'DNA Damage: A Main Determinant of Vascular Aging' by Bautista-Niño K., Portilla-Fernandez E., Vaughan D.E., Danser H.J. and Roks, A.J.M. taken from *International Journal of Molecular Sciences* 2016, 17, 748 (CC BY 4.0)[7] (p 96); Geoff Morgan (p 110); Geoff Morgan [photograph of pp. 268-269 of the book *Colour Identification Guide to Moths of the British Isles* by B. Skinner, 3rd ed., (2009 ISBN 978-87-88757-90-3), published by Apollo Books www.apollobooks.com] (p 111).

1 (CC BY-SA 3.0) https://creativecommons.org/licenses/by-sa/3.0/
2 (CC BY 2.0) http://creativecommons.org/licenses/by/2.0/
3 (CC BY 3.0) http://creativecommons.org/licenses/by/3.0/
4 (CC BY-SA 2.5) http://creativecommons.org/licenses/by-sa/2.5/
5 (CC BY-SA 2.0) https://creativecommons.org/licenses/by-sa/2.0/
6 (CC BY-ND 2.0) https://creativecommons.org/licenses/by-nd/2.0/
7 (CC BY 4.0) https://creativecommons.org/licenses/by/4.0/
8 (CC BY 2.5) http://creativecommons.org/licenses/by/2.5/

CONTENTS

INTRODUCTION

AN OVERVIEW

ONLINE

The Open University has useful tips on how to revise. Follow the link at www.brightredbooks.net

VIDEO LINK

Find out about the scientifically proven tips for effective studying by watching the clip at www.brightredbooks.net

DON'T FORGET

Keep returning to your revision notes and try to rewrite brief versions from memory to check your learning.

USING THIS BOOK FOR REVISION

In this book we have tried to present the course content in a concise form, so that you can follow the ideas and develop your own understanding. It is, however, only an **aid to your revision**. Effective revision has to be an **active process**, so your brain needs to be doing some serious work! This means that you have to:

1. take in information and think about how you can **understand it or explain it** for yourself

2. create your own revision notes using **your own words or pictures**

3. keep **returning** to your revision notes to **reinforce your learning**.

This book has lots of features to help you in your active approach to improving your understanding and your learning:

- Some words or phrases are in **bold** to emphasise their importance. These are key terms and you should be able to explain them, or be able to use them to explain other ideas.

- **Don't forget** items point out key details that might get lost in the big picture.

- We have included **online** items and **video links** which we think will help to reinforce the ideas or explain them in a different way that will help you.

- There are short **online tests** available for each topic at www.brightredbooks.net.

- **Things to do and think about** are sections that take the content of a particular page further, to help you broaden your knowledge or understanding.

COURSE STRUCTURE

The AH Biology course has three taught areas of study and an individual practical investigation.

```
                    Advanced Higher Biology
```

Cells and Proteins
This area of study focuses on the key role that proteins play in the structure and functioning of cells and organisms. The study of proteins is primarily a lab-based activity so the area of study begins with a selection of important laboratory techniques. The area of study then looks at the importance of protein structure and binding to other molecules. Conformational change of proteins is central to controlling their activity and this is studied in the context of membrane proteins, signalling between cells and in the control of cell division.

Organisms and Evolution
This area of study explores the importance of parasites in evolution. After we have introduced field techniques used for investigating evolution in the field, the area of study looks at factors influencing the rate of evolution. The maintenance of biological variation necessary to continue evolving in the 'arms race' between hosts and parasites. Sexual reproduction is central to this so we look at sex determination and mate choice. Finally, the area of study considers parasite–host interactions from a range of perspectives.

Investigative Biology
This area of study is half the size of the others and it will give you a solid grounding in the principles and practice of investigative biology in preparation for doing your own practical investigation.

The **Investigation** provides opportunities for you to put into practice the investigative skills from the taught area of study. You will need a good level of self-motivation and organisation as you develop a plan and move on to the collection and analysis of information obtained.

ONLINE

The 'syllabus' can be found at **Course Support Notes** on the SQA AH Biology website. The key areas and depth of knowledge required are listed here. Follow the link at www.brightredbooks.net

HOW THE COURSE IS GRADED

To gain a grade, you must pass the internal assessments for all three topics, sit the **written exam** and submit an **investigation report**. Your final grade is based on these marks and the grades are A, B, C or D. No grade is awarded if the marks are below those needed for a D grade.

The written exam

This lasts 3 hours and has a maximum possible 100 marks. These will be distributed approximately proportionately across the three taught units. The majority of the marks (about 70) will be awarded for **demonstration of knowledge and application of knowledge** while the other marks (about 30) will be awarded for applying **scientific inquiry and problem-solving skills**.

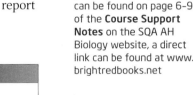

selecting information

presenting information

processing information

planning experimental procedures

making predictions

evaluating experimental procedures

drawing conclusions

The exam has two sections:

1. Section 1 has 20 multiple-choice questions, worth one mark each.

2. Section 2 has 80 marks. There will be one **short essay** (4 or 5 marks), one **long essay** (8–10 marks), a **data-handling** question (7–10 marks) and an **experimental design** question (5–9 marks). The remaining marks will be awarded to **short-answer** questions.
    The marks are scaled so that the exam is worth 75% of the total and the project report is worth 25%.

The project report

This must be a piece of individual work and your teacher/lecturer will help you to choose a suitable topic which interests you. You will research the underlying biology and carry out an open-ended investigation involving a significant amount of work that you will carry out without close supervision. For the most part, you will be working autonomously, though your teacher/lecturer will be available to provide support and advice.

Section	Marks
Abstract	1
Introduction	5
Procedures	9
Results	6
Discussion	7
Presentation	2

The final report is written up in a formal style and will be sent to the SQA for marking. The mark allocation for each section of the report is shown in the table. There are also two marks for aspects of presentation. There is more data on 'Writing Your Report' in topic 3, later in the book.

 ONLINE

More information about **the scientific inquiry and problem-solving skills** can be found on page 6–9 of the **Course Support Notes** on the SQA AH Biology website, a direct link can be found at www.brightredbooks.net

DON'T FORGET

Instead of 'essay', the SQA use the term '**extended-response question**'!

ONLINE

Get to grips with the exam format by looking at recent exam papers at www.brightredbooks.net

 THINGS TO DO AND THINK ABOUT

Broaden your interest in biology. Watch out for TV programmes on biological topics, and *NewScientist* regularly has interesting articles about cutting-edge biology. Follow biology-related Twitter accounts for up-to-the-minute news and stories.

SELECTING, PRESENTING AND PROCESSING DATA

As you progress through the Advanced Higher Biology course, you should acquire the skills to deal with complex data. Try to experience laboratory or field biology so that you become comfortable with the challenges of dealing with the variability of real data.

Below is some background to data-handling skills and some guidance on what you may be expected to do during the course. In the end, you will be expected to be able to show off a selection of these skills in your investigation, unit assessments or examination.

SELECTING INFORMATION

Data

Discrete and continuous data. Discrete data are those that naturally fall into distinct categories. Continuous data are those that vary from one extreme to another and, as a result, can be measured on a scale. Box plots show the spread of the data.

Sampled data. It is usually not possible to measure or observe every member of a population. Instead, a sample of data is collected. To be reliable, it is important to select a sample that is representative of the variation in the population as a whole – i.e. it is important that a sample is large enough to allow reliable results.

Charts

You must be able to select data from identification keys, tables, pie and bar charts, line graphs, lines of best fit, graphs with semi-logarithmic scales, graphs with error bars and information presented as box plots. Logarithmic scales increase in an exponential rather than linear manner. Each tick-mark is 10 times higher than the previous one.

Analysis

You are expected to be able to select information with reference to **three sources** at the same time. For example, you may have to find a relevant piece of information in text and use that to locate information in a table, and then use that to interpret a graph!

Statistics

Standard deviation and error bars. Standard deviation is a measure of the variability of the data. If this variability is plotted as an error bar, it allows you to judge the spread of the data that were combined in the average. Data that is very reliable has a smaller standard deviation than unreliable data.

Significance. This is the scientific measure of the likelihood or probability of a result occurring by chance. Significantly different results are difficult to explain by chance alone.

PRESENTING INFORMATION

Tables

Tabulating data is a key scientific skill and is assessed in the investigation report. Remember that the first column of data is usually the **independent variable**, and the remaining columns are raw **dependent** data and data derived from calculations.

Charts and graphs

You should be very familiar with bar charts and pie charts. These are used for discrete, rather than continuous, data.

Remember that the independent variable is plotted along the x-axis and the dependent variable is plotted up the y-axis. Make sure that the y-axis on a bar chart has a proper scale and label 0 (zero) at the origin if appropriate.

The two types of graph that you should be able to draw are the line graph and the histogram. These are both used for continuous data. The line graph is used to visualise correlations between two continuous variables. Remember that the independent variable

DON'T FORGET

Quantitative data refers to numerical results and data that are the result of making measurements. Qualitative data refers to descriptive observations.

contd

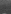

is plotted along the x-axis and the dependent variable is plotted up the y-axis. Make sure that you use proper scales along these axes and label 0 (zero) at the origin, if appropriate, on each one. For a histogram, the categories on the x-axis are convenient divisions of a continuous variable and the bars are touching.

Communication

Written communication. Science is pointless if we do not communicate the findings, so make sure that you develop great communication skills during this course. Your scientific communication is assessed in your pilot study write-up (or practical report), in your investigation and in the examination. Write clearly, coherently and logically.

Oral communication. Scientists communicate verbally at seminars, conferences and in the (coffee) bar, so make sure that you spend time in class verbalising your ideas and double-checking that you know the right vocabulary and how to use it.

PROCESSING INFORMATION

Number

You will need to be able to perform calculations using numbers in order to process data. These could involve whole numbers, decimals or fractions. In general, there are no marks for working (even when you are given space for working).

Proportion

At the heart of any science is the need to compare data, so it is important that you understand the concept of proportion and the associated mathematical tools. To compare different numbers, we use a ratio or a fraction. To compare different fractions more easily, we use percentages. A common requirement is to calculate a percentage change so remember:

$$\text{percentage change} = [(\text{final} - \text{original})/\text{original}] \times 100$$

Accuracy

It is important to consider accuracy when processing data. When calculating averages, you would not normally express the answer to more decimal places than the original data. Where it is appropriate to do so, do not go to more than one more decimal place than the original data.

Units

Units should always be stated and should be m, s, ml, kg, g, etc. Do not leave units out. Do not use imperial units. It is fine to express units using a solidus (e.g. m/s) or as scientific notation (e.g. ms^{-1}).

Remember that there are 1000 nano (n) in one micro (μ). There are 1000 μ in a milli (m). There are 1000 m in a unit. One thousand units is a kilo (k). One thousand k is mega (M), and 1000 M is giga (G).

Means and ranges

You have to be able to work out a mean average and the range of a set of data. You will not have to calculate a standard deviation in the exam, though it might be very useful in your investigation. Use spreadsheets to help you process data.

 THINGS TO DO AND THINK ABOUT

Biologists can be wrong ... sometimes. The range is properly defined as the number of units between the lowest and highest value. However, biologists usually state the **range** as the lowest to the highest value; this is really a measure of the **spread** of the data.

 DON'T FORGET

Remember that in bar charts there should be spaces between the bars – just like in jail!

 DON'T FORGET

In a histogram, plot the bars next to one another without any gaps – a histogram is a squishtogram!

 DON'T FORGET

There are no half marks in Biology.

DON'T FORGET

If there has been a decrease, then the percentage change figure will be negative. Alternatively, it can be called a percentage decrease and then the negative symbol is not required.

LABORATORY TECHNIQUES FOR BIOLOGISTS: HEALTH AND SAFETY

HAZARDS IN A LABORATORY

A hazard is anything that can cause **harm or injury to people**, or that can cause **ecological damage** if it is released from the laboratory. However, not all hazards are created equal.

Three types of hazards

1. Substances

One class of hazardous substances is the **toxic chemicals**. Lead ethanoate is an example of cumulative poison as the lead ions can bioaccumulate in the body over long periods of time and act as a non-competitive inhibitor of many enzymes. Potassium cyanide is an acute poison which works rapidly when it enters the body by acting as a competitive inhibitor of an enzyme in the electron transport chain in cellular respiration.

Another class of hazardous substance is the **corrosive chemicals**. While ethanoic acid is mildly corrosive (and safe to have on your chips), concentrated sulfuric acid is highly corrosive and can cause severe burns to exposed skin.

The last class of hazardous substance is the **flammable substances.** Sunflower oil needs to be heated to over 300°C before it ignites while ethanol is highly flammable at room temperature. Though it is not a substance, **heat** also needs to be taken into consideration as a hazard in the laboratory.

2. Organisms

Some **animals and plants can present hazards**. The New Zealand flatworm (*Arthurdendyus triangulates)* has mucus with protease enzymes so it is an irritant to human skin. When plants of the genus *Euphorbia* are damaged, they release a latex which causes severe and painful skin inflammation.

The organisms that we most commonly need to consider in the laboratory are micro-organisms. The biggest hazards are presented by the **pathogenic organisms**. However, even within one species, there can be harmless strains and virulent strains. For example, exposure to *Escherichia coli* K12 is unlikely to cause any ill effects while infection by *E.coli* 0157 is potentially lethal.

3. Equipment

The equipment used in a laboratory can also present hazards. Clearly a sharp scalpel can cause injury if not used carefully. **Mechanical equipment** can also present hazards if not used correctly. For example, the lid of a centrifuge must not be opened until the spinning has stopped as the rapidly moving rotor could cause serious injuries if touched.

CONTROL OF RISK IN A LABORATORY

Risk is defined as the **likelihood of harm** arising from **exposure to a hazard**. A crucial aspect of laboratory work is the control of risks and this is achieved by carrying out a **risk assessment**.

Risk assessment

This involves identifying **control measures** to minimise the risk posed by the hazard. The control measures do not remove the hazard – they should bring the risk down to an **acceptable level**. If it is not possible to bring the risk down to an acceptable level then the lab work cannot proceed.

Hand centrifuge

Enclosed centrifuge

The hand centrifuge on the left presents too high a risk of injury for use in a school laboratory. The control measure is to use a centrifuge with an enclosed rotor mechanism as shown in the mechanical centrifuge on the right. While the hazard is still present, the control measure greatly reduces the risk.

Examples of control measures

The control measure for each hazard needs to be considered specifically as it relates to reducing the risk from that hazard. There are three broad categories of control measures that can be used to reduce the risk from most hazards. These are:

- **appropriate handling techniques**, such as using tongs or oven mitts to handle hot objects
- **protective clothing and equipment**, such as safety glasses, protective gloves or fume cupboards to prevent exposure to a hazardous substance
- **aseptic technique** to prevent exposure to, and escape of, a pathogenic organism.

Hazard	Risk (High, med, low)	Severity (High, med, low)	Control measures (procedures, equipment, clothing, skills training)

An example of the type of headings that could be used in a risk assessment table

 THINGS TO DO AND THINK ABOUT

Think back on some of the lab work you have done in school.

What hazards were there? What control measures reduced the risks of harm?

These two cyclists know the hazards from other road users so they wear hi-viz clothing to reduce the risk. The hazard of a head injury is also reduced by wearing a helmet.

 DON'T FORGET

Risk assessment can only minimise risk, not remove risk.

 DON'T FORGET

Risk assessment can only minimise risk, not remove risk.

 ONLINE

Read an article describing some of the hazards and risks of laboratory work at www.brightredbooks.net

 VIDEO LINK

Visit the Digital Zone to watch a short view of hazardous chemicals and ways of reducing the risk from using them.

 ONLINE TEST

Test your knowledge of this topic at www.brightredbooks.net

LABORATORY TECHNIQUES FOR BIOLOGISTS: LIQUIDS AND SOLUTIONS

DILUTION SERIES

The study of cells and proteins in the laboratory requires careful development of basic laboratory skills. Many substances are found in cells at extremely low concentrations. To recreate cellular conditions in the laboratory requires an understanding of **dilution** and **measurement uncertainty**. To ensure accuracy, it is important to use appropriate measuring methods whether using scales, measuring cylinders, pipettes or autopipettes.

10^{-1} of original concentration
10^{-2} 10^{-3} 10^{-4} 10^{-5} 10^{-6}

Dilutions are used in many experimental procedures. They can be used to control potential confounding variables in an experimental system, to generate a suitable range in an independent variable or as a way of modifying the dependent variable, so that a measureable value can be obtained.

transfer
1ml   2ml   3ml   4ml   5ml   6ml
10ml total
9ml   8ml   7ml   6ml   5ml   4ml
0.1 C   0.2 C   0.3 C   0.4 C   0.5 C   0.6 C
concentration C

A linear dilution series that would make six dilutions, each with a volume of 10 ml. To calculate the volume of stock solution required (V_1) to make a new concentration (C_2) the formula $V_1C_1 = V_2C_2$ can be used. Note that in this example V_2 is always 10 ml.

Linear dilution series

A linear dilution series consists of a range of dilutions that differ by **an equal interval**. For example, solutions of concentrations 0·1, 0·2, 0·3, 0·4, 0·5 and 0·6 ml would represent a linear dilution series.

To make a linear dilution series, it is normal practice to add different volumes of stock solution to different volumes of solvent. In this way, **each concentration is made individually** and any measurement errors affect only the one concentration.

1.0 ml transfer   1.0 ml transfer   1.0 ml transfer   1.0 ml transfer   1.0 ml transfer   1.0 ml transfer
10 ml total
10^{-1} C 10^{-2} C 10^{-3} C 10^{-4} C 10^{-5} C 10^{-6} C
1.0 ml transfer
concentration C
count colonies = N
each colony grew from a single cell

A log dilution series involving six 10-fold dilutions. Note that each dilution acts as the stock to make the next dilution in the series. Log dilution series are often used to allow the estimate of microbial cell density. In the case at the top of this page, the number of colonies is countable on the 10^{-4} and 10^{-5} plates which allows the undiluted concentration of viable cells (C) in the original culture to be calculated. C = approximately 2·6 × 10^7 cells per ml.

Log dilution series

A log dilution series consists of a range of different dilutions that differ by a **constant proportion**. For example, solutions of concentrations 10^{-1}, 10^{-2}, 10^{-3}, 10^{-4}, 10^{-5} and 10^{-6} would represent a log dilution series.

To make a log dilution series, it is normal for each dilution solution to act as the stock for the subsequent dilution. In this way, each concentration depends on those made before and any earlier measurement **errors are compounded** in later dilutions.

DON'T FORGET

Any measurement errors made while making up any stock solution will be compounded if further dilutions are made.

COLORIMETER

A colorimeter is used to measure the **concentration of a pigment** in a solution, the **turbidity** of liquid or the **density of cells** in a culture. It does this by illuminating a small sample of the test substance, held in a small transparent cuvette and electronically recording how much of the light is **absorbed** by the sample. A suitable wavelength filter is used so that the concentration of a coloured solution can be determined. For turbidity, a denser sample will show a lower degree of **transmission**. For each experiment the

contd

machine is **calibrated** using a 'blank' cuvette containing solvent only, which acts as a **baseline** for the comparison.

Typical uses of a colorimeter in schools include measuring:

- the density of a cell culture growing in a liquid broth – careful aseptic technique is required for this
- the concentration of betanin leaking from beetroot cells whose membrane proteins have been denatured by heat
- the rate of reaction of enzymes such as dopa oxidase
- quantifying the result of an ELISA demonstration.

A colorimeter along with a series of cuvettes. Do not expect your colorimetry investigation to be as colourful as this!

STANDARD CURVE FOR DETERMINING AN UNKNOWN

A standard curve is made by plotting the absorbance readings for a series of **known concentrations** of a substance or culture. Once the line (the standard curve) has been produced, it can be used as a reference for any samples of unknown concentrations of the same substance or culture. Through **interpolation**, the concentration of the unknown can be estimated.

The absorbance of standard solutions of known concentration is measured in a colorimeter – in this case, 0·1, 0·2, 0·3 and 0·4 units. The standard curve is plotted using these data. The standard curve can now be used to determine the concentration of an unknown, once its absorbance has been measured. It is only possible to interpolate from a standard curve, so if the unknown appears to have a concentration outside the initial range of the standards, then a greater range of standards must be measured.

VIDEO LINK

Watch the video at www. brightredbooks.net to see a portable colorimeter in action.

VIDEO LINK

Head to www. brightredbooks.net and watch the clip for a demonstration of how to determine the molecular weight of an unknown protein after gel electrophoresis.

BUFFERS TO CONTROL PH

Buffers are aqueous solutions that show **very little variation in their pH** despite addition of acids or alkalis. As almost all biological processes are pH dependent, cells and their secretions tend to contain pH buffers. For example, in mammalian blood the presence of carbonic acid and bicarbonate anions buffers the blood pH and keeps it between the values of pH 7·35 and 7·45. Any variation beyond either pH 6·8 or 7·8 is likely to be lethal.

In laboratory experiments, buffers can be selected so that the pH of reaction mixture can be kept constant. In cell-culture media, buffers are used to prevent pH changes that could otherwise occur as a result of the build-up of waste products.

 ONLINE

There is a useful overview of risk assessment at www. brightredbooks.net

THINGS TO DO AND THINK ABOUT

Interpolate, don't extrapolate

Interpolation is the prediction of a data point between two valves and is a scientific technique that can allow confident predictions to be made.

Extrapolation involves predicting a data point beyond the last known value, and this means you'll have less confidence in the prediction.

 ONLINE TEST

Head to www. brightredbooks.net to test yourself on this topic.

LABORATORY TECHNIQUES FOR BIOLOGISTS: SEPARATION TECHNIQUES

CENTRIFUGATION

Centrifugation is a method for separating materials **in suspension** according to their **differing density**. Since almost everything within living cells is essentially in suspension, this is a suitable method for separating different cell constituents. Biological fluids require little preparation, but solid tissue is homogenised in a blender first with the addition of buffer. The material is rotated in a **centrifuge tube** at between **2000 to 120 000 revolutions per minute**. The resultant **g**-force causes the constituents to separate. The most dense components form a **pellet** at the bottom of the tube, whereas the less dense liquid fraction above is termed the **supernatant**.

cell extract

low-speed spin

high speed spin

supernatant

pellet

Careful consideration of centrifugation speed and duration results in different fractions in the pellet.

Typical uses of a centrifuge in a school setting include enzyme extractions from tissue, such as potato-starch phosphorylase; the use of centrifugation ensures that the enzyme in the supernatant is separated from any starch, which ends up in the pellet for disposal. In the study of the activity of chloroplast electron transport chains (also known as the Hill reaction), a centrifuge can be used to separate the photosynthetic membranes from other cell constituents; in this case the required fraction is the pellet and the supernatant is discarded.

Thin-layer chromatography separation of photosynthetic pigments from green plants. This result demonstrates that there are several different light-harvesting membrane pigments within the chloroplast.

CHROMATOGRAPHY

Paper and thin-layer chromatography

In paper and thin-layer chromatography, amino acids or sugars can be separated according to their characteristics of **solubility**. The materials being tested are spotted toward the base of the chromatography medium and a solvent mix pulls the different constituents up the chromatogram. The different solubilities of the materials being tested result in different speeds of movement, so the constituents travel different distances. In paper chromatography, the cellulose paper is highly hydrophilic and the solvent used has hydrophobic properties. Similar solvent properties are used in thin-layer chromatography but the thin layer is made from silica gel or cellulose.

Chromatography

Leu — least polar amino acid

Ala

Glu — most polar amino acid

origin

In the chromatography of amino acids, the chemical properties of the R-group determine the distance travelled along the chromatogram.

Affinity chromatography

Affinity chromatography is a technique for the separation of one specific soluble protein from a mixture. An **antibody or ligand** specific for binding with the protein in question is immobilised in a gel or solid matrix and packed into a column. The mixture of proteins is poured through the column. Only the target protein with a high affinity to the antibody or ligand binds within the column. The other proteins will not bind and are washed out as they have a weaker affinity. By then **washing the column** with either a buffer of different pH (which lowers the affinity of the protein to the ligand) or with a solution containing free ligand, the target protein can be recovered.

ONLINE

A thorough description of affinity chromatography is available at www. brightredbooks.net

contd

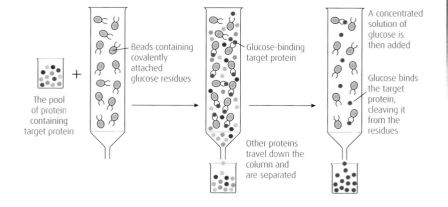

The use of affinity chromatography to separate a glucose-binding target protein from a mixture of proteins. Note that immobilised glucose residues separate the target protein from the mixture and then a concentrated solution of glucose is added to the target protein.

The pool of protein containing target protein

Beads containing covalently attached glucose residues

Glucose-binding target protein

Other proteins travel down the column and are separated

A concentrated solution of glucose is then added

Glucose binds the target protein, cleaving it from the residues

GEL ELECTROPHORESIS

Gel electrophoresis uses current flowing through a buffer to separate either proteins or nuleic acids. **Size** and **charge** are factors that affect the rate at which any macromolecule migrates through a gel. It is possible to run gels with the proteins in their native non-denatured (folded) state so their separation is by state, size and charge. Alternatively, in SDS–PAGE proteins are separated by size alone in a non-native denatured (unfolded) state. To unfold the protein, it is denatured by heat in the presence of detergent – the result is an unfolded linear protein with uniform negative charge along its length.

A SDS-PAGE electrophoresis gel of denatured muscle proteins stained with Coomasie blue so that each protein band can be visualised. The outermost lanes contain a kaleidoscope standard; these standards allow a standard curve to be plotted and the molecular weight of the other proteins to be estimated.

ISOELECTRIC POINT

The isoelectric point (IEP) of a protein is the pH at which it has **no net charge**. Above and below this pH there will either be a majority of positive or negative charges at the surface of the protein and the protein will be soluble. Water molecules interact with these charges, keeping the protein suspended in solution. At the IEP, the overall neutral charge allows the protein to form a solid and **precipitate** out of solution. This technique can be used to separate proteins from one another. By slowly changing the pH of a solution using buffers, successive proteins can be separated as only proteins with an IEP of that pH will precipitate. For example, casein in milk has an isoelectric point of pH 4.7 and will precipitate at this point.

The isoelectric point (pI) of beta-lactoglobulin is 5·3 as this is the pH at which it has an overall neutral charge (an equal number of positive and negative charges). Under these conditions the protein forms larger aggregations to precipitate.

mouse urine

Male   female

In two-dimensional gel electrophoresis, proteins are first separated by pH and then by an electric field. Each soluble protein stops migrating through the gel at its IEP in the pH gradient because it has no net charge. Then, using SDS–PAGE allows them to also be separated by size.

THINGS TO DO AND THINK ABOUT

An interesting investigation could involve the following steps. The primary sequence of a protein of interest could be found by searching an online database. Using the website isoelectric.ovh.org, the isoelectric point of the protein could be predicted. In the laboratory, the isoelectric point of the protein could be determined experimentally.

VIDEO LINK

Watch a clear demonstration of the electrophoresis of fish muscle tissue at www.brightredbooks.net

ONLINE TEST

Test yourself on this topic online at www.brightredbooks.net

LABORATORY TECHNIQUES FOR BIOLOGISTS: ANTIBODY TECHNIQUES AND MICROSCOPY

Variable region

Constant region

CDRs

Each antibody is a double-headed structure. The ends of each head are variable – this means that they differ from one specific antibody clone to another. All the antibodies produced by any one B lymphocyte are, of course, absolutely identical in structure. At the tip of the variable region, coloured in red here, is the unique arrangement of polypeptide R-groups involved in binding with the antigen. These areas are known as the complementarity determining regions.

1

2 wash

3 wash

4 wash

5 wash

This ELISA involves an antibody (1) attached to the bottom of a plastic well. If a test sample contains the specific antigen then this will bind (2) to the antibody. If an enzyme-linked antibody is then added (3), it will bind only where the antigen has bound. If the enzyme substrate is added (4), then a colour-change reaction occurs (5). It is vital that the test well is thoroughly rinsed between each stage to prevent false-positive results being obtained.

ANTIBODIES

Immunoassay techniques are powerful tools in laboratory studies for the **detection and identification of specific proteins**. The ability of antibodies to bind to specific antigens is utilised in antibody techniques.

Antibodies are Y-shaped globular proteins produced by B lymphocytes as part of the immune response of a vertebrate. Each B lymphocyte produces one specific antibody that **binds** to one specific antigen. This binding helps to render an antigen harmless, as described on page 87. The spleen and bone marrow are the sites of production of B lymphocytes.

A serum containing antibodies can be harvested from the blood of animals that have been exposed to a particular antigenic material. Some time after exposure, blood is removed and antibodies are separated by centrifugation. Many different antibodies will have formed to different parts of the antigen. Each antibody is made by a single B lymphocyte clone. A serum made in this way with many different antibodies against an antigen is described as **polyclonal**.

MONOCLONAL ANTIBODIES

Immunoassay techniques require stocks of monoclonal antibodies. To manufacture antibodies that are **identical** and will **bind to exactly the same feature of the antigen** – is an essential stage in all immunoassay techniques. To produce pure monoclonal antibodies, a single line of **lymphocytes** must be grown, each secreting the same specific antibody.

IMMUNOASSAY TECHNIQUES USING REPORTER ENZYMES

Monoclonal antibodies are used in the **diagnosis and detection of disease**. For example, **immunoassay techniques** (such as ELISA) involve the use of monoclonal antibodies that have an enzyme attached. This **reporter enzyme** catalyses a colour-change reaction that is used to detect and quantify the presence of a specific antigen. If the antigen is present, the antibody binds allowing the reporter enzyme to produce a coloured product – visual confirmation of the antigen's presence. If the antigen is not present, the antibody cannot bind and the enzyme is washed away before any reaction can take place. Rather than manufacture a specific antibody with a linked reporter enzyme for every possible antigen of interest, two antibodies are usually used. The first is specific to the antigen and the second is specific to the constant region of the first type of antibody. Blood samples can be screened for either antigens or antibodies for particular pathogens, such as HIV or meningitis. Pregnancy testing kits use the immunoassay technology to detect the presence in the urine of human chorionic gonadotrophin (HCG), a hormone only produced by the placenta. Other reporters can be used, other than enzymes, such as chemiluminesce or fluoresce.

WESTERN BLOTTING

Western blotting is a technique for **identifying specific proteins** that have been separated using SDS-PAGE gel electrophoresis. The proteins are **blotted** from the gel onto a solid medium, recording their final positions on a more convenient material.

The filter is then flooded with **fluorescent-labeled monoclonal antibodies** or other reporters. Several different antibodies can be used simultaneously, as long as each has a differently coloured fluorescent marker. Once the antibodies have bound to their target proteins, the excess is washed away. When exposed to light of particular wavelengths, the fluorescent-labeled antibodies allow the precise location of their specific target proteins to be identified. A fluorescent-labeled protein blot allows the location of the target protein to be precisely identified.

Size (kDa)

50
37
25
20
15

A western protein blot allows the location of the target protein to be precisely identified.

FLUORESCENCE MICROSCOPY

Histochemistry is the study of tissues using stains and microscopy. Fluorescent-immunohistochemical staining is a technique that is used to **visualise the distribution of specific cellular components in live cells**. In fluorescence microscopy particular protein structures can be visualised in a way that previously was not possible.

Ocular lens (eyepiece)
Reflecting prism
Objective lens
Specimen on stage
Condenser lens
Base with light source

Bright field microscopy is commonly used to examine whole organisms, parts of organisms or sections of dissected tissue or individual cells. The specimens must be small and thin enough to mount under a coverslip on slides or cavity slides. Stains are often used to improve the definition. Magnifications up to ×400 are commonly used and, with the use of oil immersion, ×1000 is possible.

Fluorescent-immunochemical staining of mouse cell telophase. The nucleosomes are fluorescing blue, the tubulin of the spindle fibres fluorescing orange and the actin cytoskeleton is fluorescing green. In each case, a specific fluorescent-labeled antibody has bound to each type of protein to show the precise location of each subcellular structure.

 THINGS TO DO AND THINK ABOUT

Monoclonal antibodies are increasingly being used in the treatment of disease. In this technology, toxins are attached to tumour-specific monoclonal antibodies. When the antibodies reach the tumour cells, they combine with their specific antigens, bringing the toxins into close contact with the target cells and killing them. If you want to find out more, research the use of the monoclonal antibody trastuzumab in cancer treatment.

 DON'T FORGET

An assay determines the presence or concentration of a substance in a mixture; an immunoassay uses a monoclonal antibody to do this.

 VIDEO LINK

Watch the description of the use of fluorescent-labeled protein blotting in research into neurodegenerative disease in Scotland at www.brightredbooks.net

 ONLINE TEST

Test yourself on this topic at www.brightredbooks.net

LABORATORY TECHNIQUES FOR BIOLOGISTS: ASEPTIC TECHNIQUES AND CELL CULTURE

ONLINE TEST

Test yourself on this topic at www.brightredbooks.net

DON'T FORGET

A cell line is a genetically uniform cell culture developed from a single cell.

ASEPTIC TECHNIQUE

Contamination is the enemy of cell culture. Aseptic technique is a set of **precautions taken to eliminate unwanted microbial contamination**. It involves the sterilisation of equipment and culture media by heat or chemical means and subsequent exclusion of microbial contamination: it is vital to prevent accidental inoculation with unwanted cells or spores. Bacterial or fungal contamination can rapidly outcompete and spoil a culture of slower-growing plant or animal cells.

Sterilise loop in Bunsen flame

Pass neck of culture bottle through flame (keep lid in hand)

Pass neck of culture bottle through flame and replace lid

Carefully touch single colony with loop

Streak an area of agar on labelled petri dish

Sterilise loop in Bunsen flame

Streak across previous streaks and sterilise loop again

Streak a third and fourth time, sterilising the loop each time. Then seal plates and incubate

An example of good aseptic technique: the stages in subculturing a microorganism from a pure colony on an agar slope. The streak plate technique is an ideal technique for the detection of contamination and should provide pure colonies for further subculture.

MICROBIAL CULTURE

Some microbes can be grown in suspension using liquid medium (broth) with suitable nutrients. Other types can be grown on, or within, a solid medium (substrate) such as agar jelly. To ensure rapid growth of the chosen cells, optimum conditions are provided in terms of nutrients, pH and gases. Anaerobic organisms can be cultured in non-aerated suspension or within agar. Many culture media exist that promote the growth of specific types of cells and microbes.

A microbial culture can be started using an **inoculum**, where growing cells are added in a volume of liquid medium from a previous culture. Touching a broth or a culture plate with a sterile loop will gather enough microbes for an inoculum.

(a)

(b)

(c)

Different organisms require different media to grow well in the laboratory. Here single colonies are isolated using streak plates: (a) *Micrococcus luteus* on nutrient agar; (b) *Vibrio cholera* on bile salt agar; (c) *Escherichia coli* on MacConkey agar.

ANIMAL CELL CULTURE

Mammalian cells are usually cultured in liquid in a flask. To undergo rapid growth and cell division in culture, most mammalian cells require the addition of a complex medium containing chemical **growth factors** from serum. The addition of an **animal serum**, such as foetal bovine serum (FBS), is essential. As well as growth factors, FBS is a mixture containing proteins, salts, vitamins and glucose. Antibiotics are added to minimise the chances of spoilage by microorganisms. Growth factors are proteins that promote cell growth and proliferation.

The cells soon use up the nutrients in the medium, so, to keep the cloned **cell line** alive, some must be subcultured into a fresh culture flask. Newly created animal cell lines

contd

(primary cell lines) tend to **die** after a finite number of divisions (about 60 – the Hayflick limit). This reduces the length of time a **primary cell-line** culture can be maintained. However, this limit does not exist in **tumour cell lines**, which are immortal and can be subcultured indefinitely, as they perform unlimited divisions.

COUNTING COLONY-FORMING UNITS

Plating out a liquid microbial culture on solid media allows the number of colony-forming units to be counted and the density of cells in the culture estimated. Serial dilution is often needed to achieve a suitable colony count.

USING HAEMOCYTOMETERS

A haemocytometer is a graduated microscope slide used to **count cell density**. It was originally designed to count the density of blood cells, hence its name. The coverslip of a haemocytometer slide is designed to sit a known distance from the slide. This means that the viewer is looking through a **known volume of medium**. By counting the number of cells in a particular area of the grid, a cell density can be calculated.

A haemocytometer can be used to make **total cell counts**, or if vital staining is used to distinguish living cells, it can be used to make **viable cell counts**. An example of a **vital stain** is methylene blue; when yeast is viewed under the microscope at high power using this stain, the vital or living cells are colourless, whereas dead cells are blue. It is often useful to know what proportion of a cell culture is viable.

Animal cell culture can either be (a) in flasks or (b) in suspension in liquid medium. In either case the cells require a complex medium containing growth factors from animal serum. Primary cell lines will have a limited lifespan but cancer cell lines can divide indefinitely, as long as they are subcultured regularly.

cell suspension

0.1 mm gap

count all cells within the 4 corner areas

1 mm

1 mm

A haemocytometer slide allows the number of cells in a known volume to be counted. If all of the cells within the four corner 1 mm² squares and the centre 1 mm² square are counted, this gives the total cell count per 0.5 mm³ of medium (as the depth is given as 0.1 mm). Consistent counting rules must be followed to prevent overestimating abundance. So, cells in contact with only two edges of the squares are considered to be within the square.

THINGS TO DO AND THINK ABOUT

Could a doctor start a cell line using your cells without your permission? Do human cell lines have 46 chromosomes? Why do some cell lines become 'laboratory weeds'? Find out more about the *HeLa* cell line to answer these questions and maybe read the bestselling book *The Immortal Life of Henrietta Lacks*.

 VIDEO LINK

Watch the tutorial in the use of haemocytometers to calculate cell density at www.brightredbooks.net

THE PROTEOME AND INTRACELLULAR MEMBRANES

DON'T FORGET

All cells in an organism have the same set of genes. Cellular differentiation is due to differences in gene expression, RNA splicing and post-translational modification to form the particular proteome of each specific tissue.

ONLINE

Read about how Glasgow University researchers used proteomics to find that raw olive oil in the diet reduces the presence of heart disease biomarkers at www.brightredbooks.net

THE PROTEOME

An organism's **genome** is its complete set of DNA, including both the protein-coding genes and the non-coding RNA genes. The latter includes those that are transcribed to produce tRNA, rRNA and RNA molecules that control expression of other genes. The number of protein-coding genes in the human genome is not accurately known and estimates vary between 20 000 to 25 000. All cells will express the important housekeeping genes (such as those for respiration and protein synthesis) but they will only express a sample of the other genes, producing the proteins characteristic for that type of cell. The set of proteins expressed by a given cell type can vary over time and under different conditions.

The **proteome** is the entire set of proteins that can be expressed from a genome. In eukaryotes in particular, this number is much larger than the number of genes. For example, the human proteome is estimated at between 250 000 and over a million different proteins. The proteome is much larger because of **alternative RNA splicing** – depending on which RNA segments are treated as exons and introns in a primary RNA transcript of a gene, different mature mRNA molecules are produced. Some factors that affect the set of proteins expressed by a given cell type are the metabolic activity of the cell, cellular stress and the response to signalling molecules.

The proteins that are produced by a cell can also change due to the effects of disease. This means that specific marker proteins in the proteome can be early indicators of conditions such as heart disease or cancer.

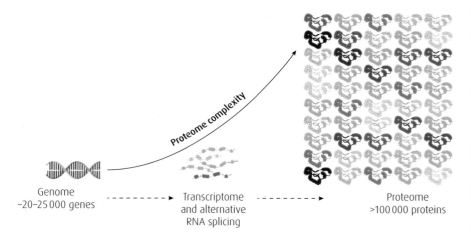

Genome
~20–25 000 genes

Transcriptome and alternative RNA splicing

Proteome
>100 000 proteins

Proteome complexity

How a genome codes for a much larger proteome.

INTRACELLULAR MEMBRANES

Cells of prokaryotes (the bacteria and Archaea) are much smaller than cells of eukaryotes (such as fungi, plants and animals). Typically, the diameter of prokaryotic cells is between 1 and 5 μm while eukaryotic cells are between 10–100 μm. The key structural difference that explains this difference in size is not the presence or absence of a nucleus but the presence or absence of intracellular membrane structures.

Prokaryotic cells

These cells do not have intracellular membrane structures in their cytoplasm. Many of the functions of these structures are carried out by the plasma membrane, so this places

contd

a limit on the maximum rate of the metabolic processes in the prokaryotic cell. This metabolic limit, in turn, restricts the maximum size that prokaryotic cells can attain.

Eukaryotic cells

Eukaryotic cells can be much larger than prokaryotic cells. This size difference means that eukaryotes have a **relatively small surface area to volume ratio**. Even the smallest eukaryotic cell has eight times the volume of the largest prokaryote but the plasma membrane is only four times larger.

This means that the plasma membrane of the eukaryote has **too small an area** to carry out all of the **vital functions** carried out by membranes. The total rate of all these processes would be too slow to provide materials to support the cell. This increase in size can only be supported because the eukaryotes have a **system of internal membranes** which **increases the total area** of membrane available for the vital metabolic processes.

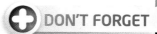

DON'T FORGET

The size of a prokaryotic cell is limited by the amount of metabolic reactions that it can carry out on its plasma membrane.

The **endoplasmic reticulum (ER)** forms a network of membrane tubules continuous with the nuclear membrane. Lipids and proteins are synthesised in the ER

Vesicles transport materials between membrane compartments or to the plasma membrane

Lysosomes are membrane - bound organelles containing a variety of hydrolase enzyme

The **Golgi apparatus** is a series of flattened membrane discs where proteins undergo post-translational modification

The system of internal membranes of an animal cell.

DON'T FORGET

The system of internal membranes in eukaryotic cells greatly increases the surface area available for the metabolic reactions carried out by membranes.

A bacterial cell, a type of prokaryote. Notice the lack of internal structures.

VIDEO LINK

Visit the Digital Zone and watch a useful video explaining the internal membrane system.

THINGS TO DO AND THINK ABOUT

The surface area of a sphere is found using the formula, $SA = 4\pi r^2$. The volume is found using $Vol = \dfrac{4}{3} \pi r^3$.

Use these formulae to check the comparison made between the largest prokaryotic cells and the smallest eukaryotic cells. If you then calculate the **surface area : volume** ratio for each, you should find that the prokaryote has 1·2 : 1 while the eukaryote only has 0·6 : 1 half the amount of membrane per unit of volume.

SYNTHESIS OF LIPIDS AND PROTEINS

SYNTHESIS OF CYTOSOLIC PROTEINS

The cytoplasm of a cell has two parts. The first part is the **cytosol** which is the liquid component of the cytoplasm. The second part is the ribosomes and the membrane-bound organelles (such as the ER, Golgi apparatus, mitochondria and chloroplast) which are suspended in the cytosol.

The synthesis of proteins for the cytosol is done entirely by **cytosolic ribosomes**. Once completed, these proteins are released from the ribosome directly into the cytosol. These proteins include the enzymes of glycolysis and the enzymes that attach amino acids to tRNA molecules for use in protein synthesis at the ribosome.

DON'T FORGET

Cytosolic proteins are synthesised entirely by ribosomes in the cytosol.

SYNTHESIS OF MEMBRANE COMPONENTS

The endoplasmic reticulum can take two forms which are connected to each other. The **rough endoplasmic reticulum** (RER) has ribosomes attached to the **cytosolic face** of its membranes. The **smooth endoplasmic reticulum** (SER) has no ribosomes attached to it.

The synthesis of **lipids** (oils, **phospholipids** and steroid hormones) is carried out by the enzymes embedded in the membranes of the SER. The phospholipids are then **inserted into the membrane** of the SER.

DON'T FORGET

Membrane lipids are synthesised in the SER.

The synthesis of **transmembrane proteins** begins at a cytosolic ribosome but it is not completed there.

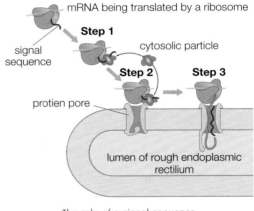

The role of a signal sequence.

- Step 1 – A polypeptide that will become part of a transmembrane protein starts with a short stretch of about 20 amino acids called a **signal sequence**. When this signal sequence emerges from the ribosome, a cytosolic particle binds to it and this **temporarily halts translation**.

DON'T FORGET

A signal sequence is a short stretch of amino acids at one end of the polypeptide that determines the eventual location of a protein in a cell.

- Step 2 – The particle also directs the ribosome to **dock with a protein pore in the ER** thus forming the rough ER.

- Step 3 – After docking, the protein pore removes the cytosolic particle and the signal sequence so translation can continue.

As it is translated, the polypeptide chain is **inserted directly into the membrane** of the ER. The ribosome is released back into the cytosol once translation is completed.

DON'T FORGET

The synthesis of all proteins begins at cytosolic ribosomes.

SYNTHESIS OF OTHER PROTEINS

Proteins that are destined for use in the mitochondria, chloroplasts or the interior of the nucleus are synthesised **entirely by cytosolic ribosomes**. After the protein has been released from the ribosome into the cytosol, these proteins have **other signal sequences** which are used to direct them to their **correct organelle**.

Polypeptides that are destined to be part of a **lysosome enzyme** or part of a **secreted protein** start their synthesis at a cytosolic ribosome and, like the transmembrane proteins, have a signal sequence that takes the ribosome to the RER. However, as they are translated through the protein pore in the RER they are **released directly into the lumen** of the RER instead of being inserted into the membrane.

MOVEMENT OF PROTEINS BETWEEN MEMBRANES

Modification in the Golgi apparatus

The polypeptides that are produced in the RER are transported by **vesicles** that bud off from the RER. The vesicles move along **microtubules** and then **fuse** with the Golgi apparatus which is a stack of hollow and flattened membrane discs. The polypeptides move through the stack of Golgi discs in vesicles that bud off from one disc and fuse to the next one in the stack.

As the polypeptides move through the stacks of discs in the Golgi apparatus, they undergo **post-translational modification**. Enzymes modify the polypeptides by catalysing the addition of **various sugars in multiple steps** to form carbohydrate groups attached to the polypeptide. The result is that the polypeptides are converted into **glycoproteins**. Most secreted proteins are glycoproteins. They are also found in the membrane where they are important for 'self' recognition by the immune system.

Leaving the Golgi apparatus

Before a protein leaves the Golgi apparatus, phosphate groups can also be added to identify its destination. **Vesicles** carrying the proteins bud off and leave the Golgi apparatus. These vesicles move along **microtubules** to other membranes and then **fuse** with them. There are four possible fates of these vesicles.

1. They can fuse with the plasma membrane to build the membrane and add transmembrane proteins.
2. They can fuse with the plasma membrane to allow a protein to be secreted (see **the secretory pathway below**).
3. They can fuse with the membranes of mitochondria, chloroplasts or nucleus to build their outer membranes and add transmembrane proteins.
4. The vesicle can form a **lysosome** in the cytosol.

Lysosomes are membrane-bound organelles containing a variety of **hydrolases** that digest proteins, lipids, nucleic acids and carbohydrates. Lysosomes digest damaged organelles to allow cells to recycle their component molecules. For example, a human liver cell recycles half of its macromolecules every week. They are also involved in **phagocytosis** by white blood cells in the immune system.

THE SECRETORY PATHWAY

Secreted proteins include peptide hormones (such as insulin) and digestive enzymes (such as pepsin). As described above, the synthesis of the polypeptides of secreted proteins starts at a cytosolic ribosome and is completed after the ribosomes have docked with the RER. Unlike the polypeptides of transmembrane proteins, the polypeptide of the secreted protein enters the lumen of the RER. The polypeptides undergo post-translational modification as they move through the discs of the Golgi apparatus and are then packaged into **secretory vesicles**. These vesicles move along microtubules to fuse with the plasma membrane, so releasing the proteins out of the cell.

So far, so similar. However, many secreted proteins are synthesised as **inactive precursors** and require **proteolytic cleavage** to produce active proteins. Insulin undergoes proteolytic cleavage in the secretory vesicle before being secreted. The digestive enzyme pepsin is secreted and then undergoes proteolytic cleavage by the acid in the stomach before it becomes active.

 THINGS TO DO AND THINK ABOUT

Can you work out why pepsin is secreted as an inactive form? The hydrochloric acid in the stomach causes the removal of a section of the inactive pepsin. This exposes the active site of the pepsin so it becomes active and can start digesting other proteins. What would happen if pepsin became active inside a cell?

Two of the fates of vesicles from the Golgi apparatus.

AMINO ACIDS

STRUCTURE OF AMINO ACIDS

Polypeptides are polymers of amino acid monomers. The amino acid sequence determines protein structure.

Amino acids have the same general structure, differing only in the R group preset. All amino acids have a central carbon atom which has four groups bonded to it: an NH_2 amine group at one side, a COOH carboxylic acid group at the other, and the remaining two bonds are taken by a hydrogen and a variable R group.

When in aqueous solution in the cell, the NH_2 group will gain a hydrogen ion to form NH_3^+ while the COOH group will lose a hydrogen ion to form COO^-.

amine group   carboxylic acid group

The structure of amino acids.

There are four classes of amino acids: **acidic, basic, polar and hydrophobic**. These classes are defined by the **functional group** of the R group and these properties are very important in the structure of proteins.

The R groups of amino acids vary in size, shape, charge, hydrogen bonding capacity and chemical reactivity. The wide range of functions carried out by proteins results from the diversity of R groups.

Amino acid class	acidic (negatively-charged)	basic (positively-charged)	polar	hydrophobic
Example of functional group in R group	—COOH	—NH_2	—OH	hydrocarbon
Example	aspartic acid	lysine	serine	alanine

Because the R groups also interact with the aqueous solutions of the cell, the carboxylic acid groups will become negatively charged (COO^-), while the basic NH_2 groups will become positively charged (NH_3^+).

Polar R groups (e.g. OH), have groups which are very slightly charged, so can form hydrogen bonds with other molecules such as water.

Hydrophobic R groups carry no charge so do not form any hydrogen bonds with water, hence they do not mix readily with water.

LINKING AMINO ACIDS

Amino acid monomers are linked together during translation at the ribosome. An enzyme causes a **condensation** reaction between two adjacent amino acids. A water molecule is removed by joining the OH of the COOH of one amino acid to a hydrogen from the NH_2 of the other amino acid. The bond that links the amino acids is called a **peptide bond**.

A condensation reaction forming a peptide bond.

Because they are all linked by peptide bonds, a chain of amino acids is called a **polypeptide**. The chain has an NH_2 group at the **N-terminus**, and a COOH at the **C-terminus**. The order in which the amino acids are synthesised into a polypeptide chain from N-terminus to C-terminus is called the **primary structure**.

The primary structure of a small polypeptide. Can you identify the classes of amino acids?

THINGS TO DO AND THINK ABOUT

The pH of a protein's environment affects the ionisation of the acidic and basic R groups and, depending on their position, these groups can be easy or difficult to ionise. Solutions of different pH affect the overall charge on a protein and are used as part of the electrophoresis and isoelectric separation techniques.

PROTEIN STRUCTURE

PRIMARY STRUCTURE

The primary structure is the sequence in which the amino acids are synthesised into the polypeptide. This amino-acid sequence determines the protein structure and, hence, the function of the protein.

Primary sequence of anti-diuretic hormone. This small polypeptide travels in the blood and has amino acids that are polar (green) and basic (blue) and which help it to mix with the aqueous plasma.

SECONDARY STRUCTURE

Secondary structure is stabilised by **hydrogen bonds** along the backbone of the polypeptide strand. These hydrogen bonds exist **between different peptide bonds** in the chain: the hydrogen of the N–H has a weak positive charge, so it is electrically attracted to the weak negative charge on the oxygen of the C=O of another peptide bond.

There are three types of secondary structure.

- The **α-helix** is a spiral with the R groups sticking outwards.

- The **β-pleated sheet** has parts of the polypeptide chain running alongside each other to form a corrugated sheet, with the R groups sitting above and below. The **β-pleated sheet** are usually **antiparallel β-pleated sheet** (chains in **opposite directions** with respect to N–C polarity) but they can also be **parallel β-pleated sheets** (chains in the **same direction** with respect to N–C polarity).

- The polypeptide chain can also form **turns** where the chain folds back on itself.

α-helix   β-pleated sheet (antiparallel)

Secondary structure, showing an **α-helix**, and a **β-pleated sheet** with a **turn**. Dotted lines show hydrogen bonds between NH and C=O.

TERTIARY STRUCTURE

The **final folded shape** of the polypeptide is called the tertiary structure. This three-dimensional conformation contains regions of secondary structure which are stabilised in position by **interactions between R groups** of amino acids. The R groups may have been far apart in the primary structure but the folding at the secondary level brings some R groups close enough to interact.

Possible interactions between the R groups are shown in the table below.

Interactions between R groups	Description
hydrophobic interactions	As a polypeptide folds into its functional shape, the hydrophobic R groups are repelled by water and so usually end up to the inside of the polypeptide.
ionic bonds	COOH and NH_2 groups ionise to become COO^- and NH_3^+. These groups are strongly charged, so attract each other.
London dispersion force	Very weak attractions between the electron clouds of atoms.
hydrogen bond	Strong attractions between molecules containing bonds O—H or N—H.
disulphide bridges	Covalent bonds form between sulfur-containing R groups.

contd

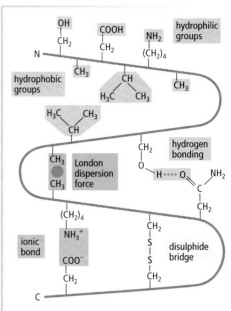

The interactions between R groups in tertiary structure.

These interactions can be affected by changes in temperature and pH. A higher temperature will cause the structure to become destabilised, disrupting the interactions that hold the protein in shape and leading to denaturation. The increased heat provides more kinetic energy and so the polypeptide chain shakes more, breaking the weaker ionic bonds, London dispersion forces and hydrogen bonds. The protein begins to unfold, eventually becoming denatured.

Changes in pH affect the ionisation of the acidic and basic R groups, changing the charge that they carry, so they no longer bond correctly and the polypeptide unfolds. As pH increases or decreases from the optimum, the normal ionic interactions between charged groups are lost, which gradually changes the conformation of the protein until becomes denatured.

Quaternary structure of collagen protein with three polypeptide chains.

QUATERNARY STRUCTURE

Many proteins have more than one polypeptide subunit which connect by bonding between their R groups. For example, collagen is made of three polypeptide subunits. Some proteins, such as lysozyme or myoglobin, have only one polypeptide chain so the tertiary structure is the final level of the structure. Quaternary structure describes the spatial arrangement of the subunits.

PROSTHETIC GROUPS

In addition to the four levels of protein structure, some proteins can also have a **prosthetic group**. This is a non-protein group which is **tightly bound** to a polypeptide unit and it is essential for the protein's function. For example, myoglobin in muscle has a complex haem group which helps to draw oxygen into the muscle cells from the blood.

Myoglobin showing tertiary structure (blue) and the haem prosthetic group (grey) with oxygen attached (red).

 ## THINGS TO DO AND THINK ABOUT

Most solids become liquid when they are warmed. So why does the egg-white protein, albumin, go solid when it is heated? The energy from the heat shakes the polypeptide chain and breaks all the weaker bonds of the secondary and tertiary structure so the hydrophobic R groups are exposed. The protein chains are now repelled by water and so clump together forming a solid mass.

Try adding strong acid to egg white – can you explain the effects? And what about whisking egg white – why does that change the protein structure?

LIGAND BINDING CHANGES THE CONFORMATION OF A PROTEIN

LIGANDS AND BINDING

Ligand is the general term for any substance that can bind to a protein. The binding of a ligand slightly changes the shape of the protein. How does this binding happen? And why is it important?

How ligand binding happens

The folding that produces the tertiary structure of a protein is stabilised by interactions between the R groups. However, there are many R groups that are not involved in the protein folding and these R groups may be exposed to the outer surface of the protein, facilitating binding to other molecules.

The protein folding produces **ligand-binding sites** on the surface of the protein. These binding sites are clefts in the surface of the globular protein which have a **complementary shape** to their ligand – they match the shape a bit like a jigsaw piece.

The binding site does more than match the shape of the ligand; it also has **complementary chemistry** to the ligand. The binding site has charged, polar and non-polar R groups arranged in it which match the charged, polar and non-polar areas on the ligand. The matched areas on the protein and the ligand interact, binding the ligand to the protein.

A ligand (black) binds to a protein. The numbers show the positions of the amino acids in the primary sequence of the protein. The ligand is interacting with the R group of Met-318 (hydrogen bonding) and with a hydrophobic non-polar pocket created by R groups of four other amino acids.

Why ligand binding is important

The interactions between the ligand and the binding site pull the polypeptide structure in towards the ligand, bringing about a change in shape – **conformational change**. The shape a protein is crucial to its function, so a change in conformation causes **functional change** in protein. Conformational change is the mechanism used to regulate the activity of proteins and is a recurring theme in the rest of this unit.

A ligand (light blue) binds to a protein, causing a conformational change and a functional change.

ALLOSTERIC INTERACTIONS

Allosteric is a term that means 'other shape' and refers to proteins that have interactions between spatially distinct sites on the same protein.

Modulation of allosteric enzymes

Modulators regulate the activity of the enzyme when they bind the allosteric site. Following binding of a modulator, the conformation of the enzyme changes and this alters the **affinity of the active site** for its substrate, thereby altering the effectiveness of substrate binding and enzyme activity. Positive modulators increase the enzyme's affinity

contd

for the substrate and so increase enzyme activity, whereas negative modulators decrease the enzyme's affinity and therefore its activity.

Cooperativity in allosteric enzymes

Many allosteric proteins consist of multiple subunits (have quaternary structure). They may show cooperativity in binding, in which binding at one subunit alters the affinity of the remaining subunits. The binding of a substrate molecule to one active site of an allosteric enzyme increases the affinity of the other active sites for binding of subsequent substrate molecules. This is of biological importance because the activity of allosteric enzymes can vary greatly with small changes in substrate concentration.

Allosteric enzymes contain a second type of site, called an allosteric site.

Cooperativity in haemoglobin

Without cooperativity, the oxygen saturation of haemoglobin would increase in a straight line as the oxygen concentration in the tissue increased. However, the oxygen dissociation curve is S-shaped, showing that the haemoglobin holds less oxygen in low oxygen surroundings and holds more oxygen in high oxygen surroundings. How can this happen?

Haemoglobin has four polypeptide subunits, each with an oxygen binding site. When an oxygen molecule binds to one subunit, it changes the conformation of the subunit. This changes the conformation of the other subunits, increasing the affinity of the other subunits for oxygen. Because the oxygen affinity of a haemoglobin molecule increases further as oxygen binds to each subunit, oxygen collection is maximised where oxygen levels are high (in the lungs or gills).

Conversely, the release of an oxygen molecule from one subunit decreases the oxygen affinity of the other subunits. In low oxygen areas (in working tissues) the release of oxygen from each subunit decreases the oxygen affinity of the other subunits, thus maximising the release of oxygen where it is needed.

The binding of oxygen to haemoglobin is influenced by temperature and pH, and these effects have physiological importance.

Hard working tissues generate heat. They also produce carbon dioxide, which reacts with water to form carbonic acid. The **increase in temperature and decrease in pH** cause the haemoglobin to have a **lower affinity for oxygen**, so the binding of oxygen is reduced. Reduced pH and increasing temperature in actively respiring tissue will reduce the binding of oxygen to haemoglobin, promoting increased oxygen delivery to tissue.

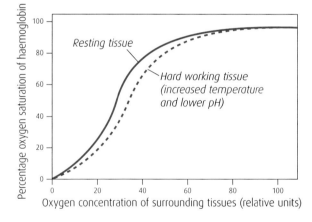

Oxygen dissociation curves. Compare the two lines at an oxygen concentration of 40 relative units – more oxygen is released from the haemoglobin to the hard working tissue.

THINGS TO DO AND THINK ABOUT

Catalase enzyme is one of the most active enzymes and it shows cooperativity, so that it can rapidly remove the harmful hydrogen peroxide which has been made as a by-product of nucleotide synthesis. When hydrogen peroxide binds to one subunit of catalase, the other three subunits become active; there are now four active sites available to quickly break down hydrogen peroxide to water and oxygen.

REVERSIBLE BINDING OF PHOSPHATE AND THE CONTROL OF CONFORMATION

ALTERING PROTEIN ACTIVITY

A large subset of proteins is inactive when they are first synthesised and require **post-translational modification** to become activated. The most common form of activation is the reversible **addition of a phosphate** on to the –OH of particular R groups (on serine, threonine or tyrosine). This phosphate can later be removed from the protein.

The addition or removal of a phosphate is used to cause **reversible conformational changes** in proteins and is an important method of **regulating the activity** of many cellular proteins, such as enzymes and receptor molecules. This ability to control protein activity is critical for signal transduction.

Adding a phosphate group adds negative charges. Ionic interaction in the unphosphorylated protein can be disrupted and new ones created.

DON'T FORGET

The addition or removal of a phosphate can **activate** or **inactivate** a protein depending on how the conformation of the protein is changed.

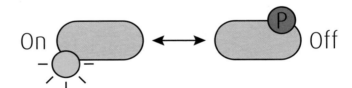

Phosphorylation can activate some proteins and deactivate others.

Protein kinases and protein phosphatases

The addition and removal of a phosphate from a protein is carried out by enzymes.

1. Protein kinases catalyse **phosphorylation**, which is the transfer of a phosphate group from ATP to other proteins. There are over 500 protein kinases in the human proteome.

2. Protein phosphatases catalyse **dephosphorylation**, which is the removal of a phosphate from a molecule and the reverse reaction of the protein kinase. There are about 150 protein phosphatases in the human proteome.

Most protein kinases are dephosphorylated and inactive. They are activated by phosphorylation – by another kinase! This reversibility of kinase phosphorylation is important in **signal transduction cascades**, where kinases activate other downstream kinases to amplify a signal. Kinases and phosphatases are also crucial in the control of the cell cycle.

DON'T FORGET

Kinases add phosphate on (KAPO), phosphatases encourage phosphate away (PEPA).

ONLINE

Hyperactive protein kinases are involved in cancers so kinase inhibitors are a major field of research. Find out about the many potential drugs that are in development at www.brightredbooks.net

contd

Phosphatase and kinase action.

ONLINE TEST

Head to www.
brightredbooks.net to test
yourself on the reversible
binding of phosphate.

ATPASES HYDROLYSE ATP

ATPases are a group of transmembrane enzymes that hydrolyse ATP and use the phosphate to **phosphorylate themselves**, rather than their substrate. The phosphate binding changes their conformation and so alters their function. The conformational change moves substancesacross the membrane. All transmembrane ATPases are involved in active transport of ions across the membrane, and the sodium–potassium pump (Na$^+$/ K$^+$ ATPase) is an important example of this type of enzyme.

 THINGS TO DO AND THINK ABOUT

The ATP synthase enzyme found in mitochondria and in chloroplasts usually harnesses a proton gradient to regenerate ATP. However, like most enzymes, ATP synthase can work in reverse. This means that it can act as an ATPase, using the binding of a phosphate from ATP to pump protons against their concentration gradient.

MEMBRANE PROTEINS

ONLINE

Visit www.brightredbooks.net for videos and further reading on this topic!

FLUID MOSAIC MODEL OF CELL MEMBRANES

The membranes of cells are made of a **phospholipid bilayer** with globular proteins penetrating the bilayer or attached to its surface. This is called the **fluid-mosaic model of membrane structure** – the phospholipid bilayer can move so it is fluid, and the separate proteins are like the small pieces of a mosaic.

A phospholipid molecule has a hydrophilic head and hydrophobic tails. The phospholipids form a bilayer with the hydrophilic heads towards the aqueous cytoplasm and the aqueous external fluid, and the hydrophobic tails to the inside of the bilayer.

MOVEMENT OF MOLECULES ACROSS MEMBRANES

The proteins in the membrane can be arranged in one of two ways.

The fluid-mosaic model of membrane structure.

- **Integral proteins** penetrate the hydrophobic interior of the phospholipid bilayer and are folded so that they have regions of hydrophobic R groups. These form **strong hydrophobic interactions**, which hold integral membrane proteins within the phospholipid bilayers. Integral membrane proteins interact exclusively with the hydrophobic region of membrane phospholipids. Some integral proteins only extend partly into the bilayer, while others are **transmembrane proteins** that span the width of the membrane.

- **Peripheral proteins** are not embedded in the phospholipid bilayer. Instead they have hydrophilic R groups on their surface and are bound to the surface of membranes, mainly by ionic and hydrogen bond interactions. Many peripheral proteins interact with the surfaces of integral membrane proteins. Some peripheral proteins on the inside of the membrane are attached to the cytoskeleton, which helps to give mechanical support and shape to the cells.

The hydrophobic centre of the phospholipid bilayer allows oxygen and carbon dioxide to pass through directly because they are **small non-polar molecules**.

The phospholipid bilayer is a barrier to **ions** (e.g. H^+, Na^+, amino acids) and most uncharged **polar molecules** (e.g. water or glucose).

Any ion or polar molecule that can pass across the membrane can only do so through a specific channel protein or transporter protein. For example, there are **specific transmembrane proteins** that act as sodium channels, glucose transporters or proton pumps.

To perform specialised functions, different cell types have different channel and transporter proteins.

Channel proteins

The passage of ions or molecules through channel proteins requires no change to the conformation of the protein channel. This is an example of **facilitated diffusion** because the proteins make it easier for the ion or molecule to move passively across the membrane. Most channel proteins in animal and plant cells are highly selective.

Channel protein in cross-section, showing the key hydrophilic R groups in the pore that let water (in this case) pass through.

Channels are multi-subunit proteins with the subunits arranged to form water-filled pores that extend across the membrane.

DON'T FORGET

Integral proteins interact with the hydrophobic interior of the membrane. Peripheral proteins form weak bonds to the surface of the membrane.

contd

Some channel proteins can be opened to allow diffusion of their ion, or closed to prevent diffusion of their ion – they are described as **gated channels** and there are two types.

Ligand-gated channels	Voltage-gated channels
Signal molecules bind to the ligand-gated channel protein and change its conformation.	If there is a large enough change in the ion concentrations across the membrane, this can change the conformation of a voltage-gated channel protein.
For example, to pass a signal on at a synapse, a neurotransmitter binds to a ligand-gated channel protein to trigger it to **open** and let Na⁺ ions flow through.	In the transmission of a nerve impulse along a nerve, the movement of ions across the membrane causes the voltage across the membrane to reach a critical level, so sodium channels **open**. The voltage change continues as more ions move across the membrane, which causes the channel to **close** again.
In rods and cones in the retina, a ligand keeps a sodium channel **closed** until light activates a pathway to release the ligand and the channels lets ions through to generate a signal.	

+ DON'T FORGET

Both types of gated channel open or close because the conformation of the protein is changed.

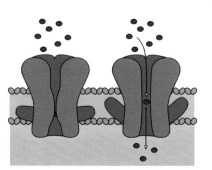

Ligand-gated channel being opened by the binding of a neurotransmitter ligand.

Voltage-gated channel being opened by a change in voltage across the membrane.

+ DON'T FORGET

Transporter proteins undergo conformational change.

Transporter proteins

Transporter proteins bind to the ions or molecules to be transported, causing the protein to undergo a **conformational change** – the proteins actually pass the ions or molecules across the membrane, rather than just providing a route through. Transporters alternate between two conformations so that the binding site for a solute is sequentially exposed on one side of the bilayer, then the other.

Active transport uses pump proteins that transfer substances across the membrane against their concentration gradient. A source of metabolic energy is required for active transport. Pumps that mediate active transport are transporter proteins coupled to an energy source.

Some active transport proteins hydrolyse ATP directly to promote the energy for the conformational change required to move substances across the membrane.

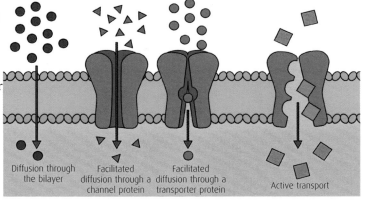

Diffusion through the bilayer — Facilitated diffusion through a channel protein — Facilitated diffusion through a transporter protein — Active transport

Diffusion is a passive process, requiring no ATP. Active transport needs ATP. Facilitated diffusion is the passive transport of substances across the membrane through specific transmembrane proteins.

💭 THINGS TO DO AND THINK ABOUT

For many years, students were told that **all** small molecules can pass directly through the phospholipid bilayer. Along with oxygen and carbon dioxide, it used to be said that water was small enough to pass through despite the fact that the phospholipids are **hydrophobic**! Water obviously needs a protein pore so how did this myth survive for so long?

Paradoxically, it was very difficult to identify this protein (now called **aquaporin**) because it is so utterly common. All cells need to allow water to pass across its membrane so there was no easy way to find a special protein when all cells have it. The discovery of aquaporin was awarded the Nobel Prize in 2003 in recognition of the challenge that had been overcome.

✓ ONLINE TEST

Head to www.brightredbooks. net and test yourself on this topic.

ION TRANSPORT PUMPS AND GENERATION OF ION GRADIENTS

For a solute carrying a net change, the concentration gradient and the electrical potential difference combine to form the electrochemical gradient that determines the transport of the solute. Ion pumps, such as the sodium–potassium pump, use energy from the hydrolysis of ATP to establish and maintain ion gradients. A membrane potential (an electrical potential difference) is created when there is a difference in electrical charge on the two sides of the membrane.

THE MIGHTY SODIUM–POTASSIUM PUMP

The sodium–potassium pump (**Na$^+$/K$^+$ ATPase**) is a vital **transmembrane transporter protein** found in most animal cells. The pump does **active transport**, moving sodium ions (Na$^+$) out of cells and potassium ions (K$^+$) into cells against steep concentration gradients by using energy directly from ATP hydrolysis.

How it works

The sodium–potassium pump has **two stable conformational states**, one with a high affinity for sodium ions inside the cell, the other with a high affinity for potassium ions outside the cell. For each ATP hydrolysed three sodium ions are transported out of the cell (3 Na$^+$ out) and two potassium ions are transported into the cell (2 K$^+$ in) to generate the electrochemical **gradients** (both concentration gradient and an electrical gradient) across the membrane.

Stage 1: In the first conformational state, the transporter protein has its ion binding sites exposed to the cytoplasm. The protein has a **high affinity for sodium ions** and **three Na$^+$ ions bind** to the binding sites.

Stage 2: When the sodium ions are attached, the transporter protein is able to **hydrolyse ATP** to ADP and phosphate ATPases hydrolyse ATP. The phosphate attaches to the protein to **phosphorylate** it and this causes a **conformational change** to the protein.

Stage 3: This new conformation has its ion binding sites exposed to the outside of the cell. Because it now has a **decreased affinity for the sodium ions**, Na$^+$ ions are released outside the cell.

Stage 4: The new conformation has a **high affinity for potassium ions** and **two K$^+$ ions bind** to the sites that are exposed to the outside of the cell. This triggers **dephosphorylation** – the release of the phosphate group from the protein.

Stage 5: This dephosphorylation causes the protein to revert to its **original conformation** with the binding sites exposed to the cytoplasm.

Stage 6: This conformation has a **low affinity for potassium ions** so K$^+$ ions are released into the cell. The transporter protein has a high affinity for sodium ions again, so the cycle is back to Stage 1 and can repeat.

DON'T FORGET

All animals rely on sodium–potassium pump pumping **2-K-in** (toucan).

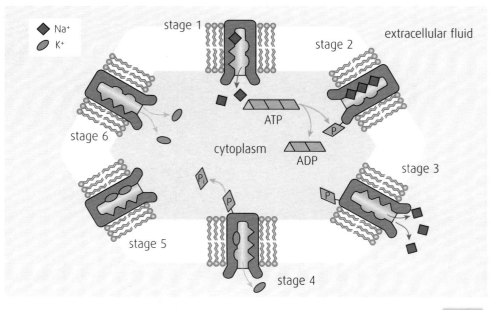

contd

Why the sodium-potassium pump is so important

The sodium–potassium pump is found in most animal cells and it accounts for a high proportion of the basal metabolic rate in many organisms.

Areas of importance include:

1. Generation and maintenance of **ion gradients for resting potential in neurons.** See pages 38–39.

2. Glucose transport in the small intestine. In the small intestine, the sodium–potassium pump generates a sodium ion gradient across the plasma membrane of intestinal epithelial cells. This then drives the active transport of glucose.

   The glucose transporter responsible for this **glucose symport** transports sodium ions and glucose at the same time and in the same direction. As the sodium ions enter the cell down their concentration gradient, the simultaneous transport of glucose pumps glucose into the cell against its concentration gradient.

VIDEO LINK

Visit www.brightredbooks.net and watch a video on the sodium-potassum pump.

ONLINE TEST

Test your knowledge of this topic at www.brightredbooks.net

THINGS TO DO AND THINK ABOUT

The mighty sodium-potassium pump maintains the concentrations of sodium and potassium ions inside the cell. This means that it is always active in cells and its action makes up a sizeable component of your metabolism. Most cells will use about 30% of the ATP they generate just powering the pump. In nerve cells, this could be up to 70%. This is why the sodium-potassium pump makes up about 25% of your BMR.

The familiar foxglove (*Digitalis purpurea*) is a very toxic species of plant to humans. It contains the poisonous compounds digoxin and digitoxin which both act as inhibitors of the sodium–potassium pump. This inhibition can lead to heart failure but in lower doses these chemicals can have therapeutic benefits in the treatment of the very same condition, as the effect of the cardiac glycosides at low concentrations is to strengthen rather than weaken the heartbeat.

COMMUNICATION AND HYDROPHOBIC SIGNALS

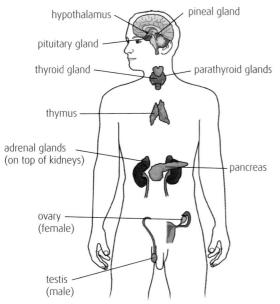

hypothalamus

pineal gland

pituitary gland

thyroid gland

parathyroid glands

thymus

adrenal glands
(on top of kidneys)

pancreas

ovary
(female)

testis
(male)

The main hormone-secreting endocrine glands in the human body. Each gland releases one or more specific signal molecule. Only certain tissues contain cells with the specific receptor proteins for these molecules. In this way, multiple signalling events can occur simultaneously. For example, the pancreas can release insulin, the pituitary gland can release anti-diuretic hormone and the thyroid can release thyroxine all at the same time, but the different target cells only respond to their intended message.

DON'T FORGET

A hydrophobic signalling molecule is able to pass through membranes. A hydrophilic signalling molecule cannot.

COORDINATION

In a multicellular organism, it is essential that cells communicate with one another. Without this communication the integration and coordination of cellular activities would be impossible. To achieve this communication, cells use **extracellular signalling molecules** and complementary **receptor proteins**.

Examples of extracellular signalling molecules are steroid hormones, peptide hormones and neurotransmitters.

The same series of events occurs whatever the details of the signal, the target or the intended response. First, the target cells must have **receptor molecules** with a **binding site** for the **specific signal molecule**. When binding occurs, it **changes the conformation of the receptor**. This change in conformation **changes the behaviour of the target cell** in some way and this initiates a **response** within the cell.

Different cell types produce **specific signals** that can only be detected and responded to by cells with the **specific receptor**. In a multicellular organism, different cell types may show a **tissue-specific response** to the same signal. Signalling molecules may have different effects on different target cell types due to differences in the intracellular signalling molecules and pathways that are involved.

Hormones

Hormones are extracellular signalling molecules that are secreted by one tissue (such as an endocrine gland) into the blood. The hormone circulates in the bloodstream until it reaches the receptor protein of its target cell or until it is broken down. Hormones are either **hydrophobic**, such as the steroid hormones oestrogen and testosterone, or are **hydrophilic**, such as peptide hormones.

Neurotransmitters

The signals that are released into the synaptic gap between a nerve cell and its neighbour are called **neurotransmitters**. Nervous communication is very specific and rapid due to the intimate association between the signalling cell and its target cell. Neurotransmitters are hydrophilic signalling molecules.

Location of receptor proteins

Hydrophobic signalling molecules can **pass through membranes**, so their receptor molecules are **within the cytoplasm or nucleus** of the target cell. Hydrophilic signalling molecules cannot pass through membranes so require integral **cell-surface receptor proteins**.

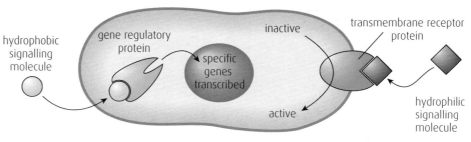

hydrophobic signalling molecule

gene regulatory protein

specific genes transcribed

inactive

active

transmembrane receptor protein

hydrophilic signalling molecule

A summary of the two signal transduction pathways.

HYDROPHOBIC SIGNALS

Hydrophobic signals and control of transcription

Hydrophobic signalling molecules include the **steroid hormones** oestrogen and testosterone. Hydrophobic signalling molecules are lipid soluble, so they are able to diffuse directly through the phospholipid bilayers of membranes, and so bind to intracellular receptors. The **receptors** for these signals are, therefore, in the cytosol or **within the nucleus** of the target cell. The receptor proteins for steroid hormones are transcription factors. Transcription factors are proteins that when bound to DNA can either stimulate or inhibit initiation of transcription. Once the hormone signal has bound to the receptor, the hormone–receptor complex is formed. This can then bind to specific sites and affect gene expression. The hormone–receptor complex binds to specific DNA sequences called hormone–response elements (HRES). Binding at these sites influences the rate of transcription, with each steroid hormone affecting the gene expression of many different genes.

As a result, hydrophobic signals can **directly influence transcription** of genes.

VIDEO LINK

Watch about steroid hormone signal transduction at www. brightredbooks.net

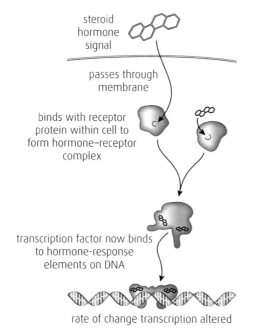

steroid hormone signal

passes through membrane

binds with receptor protein within cell to form hormone–receptor complex

transcription factor now binds to hormone-response elements on DNA

rate of change transcription altered

Mode of action of steroid hormone. Steroid signal is hydrophobic so can pass through membrane to interact with receptor proteins within the cell. Once the signal molecules bind with their receptor proteins, the proteins change conformation and form a hormone–receptor complex. This complex is a transcription factor that can now bind with the DNA and cause transcription to occur.

ONLINE TEST

Test yourself on this topic at www.brightredbooks.net

THINGS TO DO AND THINK ABOUT

When transcription factors bind, they cause DNA to have lower affinity for histone proteins, so nucleosomes unwind allowing transcription to occur.

HYDROPHILIC SIGNALS

SIGNAL TRANSDUCTION

Hydrophilic signalling molecules, such as **peptide hormones** and **neurotransmitters**, are not lipid soluble. Hydrophilic signals cannot cross the hydrophobic part of the plasma membrane, they must instead bind to **transmembrane receptor molecules** and do not enter the cytosol. These **transmembrane proteins** change conformation when the signal ligand binds to the extracellular cell surface; **the signal molecule does not enter the cell** but the **signal is transduced** across the plasma membrane. This means that the behaviour of the cell changes in response to the external binding of the signal molecule to the receptor molecule. The extracellular ligand-binding event is converted into intracellular signals.

Transduced hydrophilic signals often involve **G-proteins** or **cascades of phosphorylation by kinase enzymes**. G-proteins relay signals from activated receptors (receptors that have bound a signalling molecule) to target proteins such as enzymes and ion channels.

Phosphorylation cascades allow more than one intracellular signalling pathway to be activated. Phosphorylation cascades involve a series of events with one kinase activating the next in the sequence and so on. Phosphorylation cascades can result in the **phosphorylation of many proteins** as a result of the signalling extent.

Peptide hormones are small hydrophilic proteins. Well known examples include **insulin**, glucagon, somatotrophin (growth hormone) and anti-diuretic hormone (ADH). Each one requires a specific receptor at its target cell surface. Since only target cells have the appropriate receptors at their surface, the action of these hormones is highly specific.

Examples of **neurotransmitters** include acetylcholine (ACh) and noradrenaline. Both are hydrophilic peptides. ACh is the transmitter at the neuromuscular junction connecting motor nerves to muscles. Noradrenaline has a role in the central nervous system and the sympathetic nervous system.

Signal molecule	Lipid soluble	Passes through phospholipidic bilayer	Receptor proteins	Examples
Hydrophilic	No	No	Transmembrane protein	Peptide hormone / Neurotransmitter
Hydrophobic	Yes	Yes	In cytosol or nucleus	Steroid hormone (oestrogen, testosterone)

INSULIN AND THE RECRUITMENT OF GLUT4

Blood glucose level must be kept within narrow limits, between 3.9 and 6.1 mmol per litre of blood. The **peptide** hormones **insulin** and glucagon interact in a negative feedback system to control blood glucose level. If the blood glucose level rises, for example after a meal, the pancreas detects the increase **in blood glucose**. This causes it to increase the secretion of **insulin**.

The **insulin receptor** is a **kinase-linked receptor** found in the cell membrane of fat and muscle cells. Once the peptide hormone insulin binds to its receptor, the signal is transduced and a series of **phosphorylation events** (an intracellular signalling cascade) that triggers the **recruitment of GLUT4 glucose transporters** to the cell membrane. These transporters allow glucose to enter these cells for further metabolism and the blood glucose concentration is controlled.

Diabetes mellitus is a medical condition caused by a deficiency in the effect of insulin and results in the loss of control of blood glucose level. It can be caused by **failure to produce insulin (Type 1)** or **loss of receptor function (Type 2)**. Type 1 diabetes is treated with injections of insulin. However, in Type 2 diabetes cells are no longer sensitive to insulin and this disease is generally associated with obesity. **Exercise** reduces the impact of Type 2 diabetes as it **triggers recruitment of GLUT4** through other metabolic pathways; **exercise improves the uptake of glucose** to fat and muscle cells in subjects with Type 2 disease.

When blood glucose is high, insulin is produced. Hydrophilic, it must bind to the receptor at cell surface. The signal is transduced and a cascade of kinase-catalysed phosphorylation results in the recruitment of a vesicle to the cell surface. This vesicle is studded with GLUT4 glucose-transporter proteins. As soon as the vesicle becomes part of the cell membrane, glucose can enter the cell.

 THINGS TO DO AND THINK ABOUT

Since the 1923 Nobel Prize for medicine was awarded to Banting and Macleod, many Nobel prizes have been awarded for research into aspects of cell signalling. To get a flavour of some of the challenges, rivalries and successes involved in the discovery of insulin, watch the feature film *Glory Enough for All*.

 VIDEO LINK

Watch the animations about insulin, insulin receptors and diabetes at www. brightredbooks.net

 ONLINE TEST

Test yourself on hydrophilic signals at www.brightredbooks.net

NERVE IMPULSE TRANSMISSION

RESTING POTENTIAL OF NEURONS

Resting membrane potential is a state where there is no net flow of ions across the membrane.

The sodium–potassium pump moves three positively charged Na$^+$ ions out of a neuron cell and two positively charged K$^+$ ions into the neuron cell. The neuron membrane also has potassium channels which let some of the K$^+$ ions leak back out of the cell, and the result is a positive charge outside the cell compared to inside the cell. The transmission of a nerve impulse along a neuron requires changes in the membrane potential of the neuron's plasma membrane.

Triggering an action potential

An action potential is a wave of electrical excitation along a neuron's plasma membrane.

Depolarisation of the resting potential can be triggered by **neurotransmitter molecules** (e.g. acetyl choline) at a synapse. The neurotransmitter binds to a **transmembrane receptor protein** on the surface of the next neuron. This receptor is a **ligand-gated ion channel** so the binding of the neurotransmitter causes a change in conformation, making the channel open and letting Na$^+$ ions diffuse through.

If **sufficient ion movement** occurs, then the voltage change across the membrane reaches a **critical level** and a patch of membrane is **depolarised**. This voltage change causes the neighbouring **voltage-gated Na$^+$ channel** to open, which depolarises neighbouring regions of membrane and leads to a domino effect: the triggering of one voltage-gated channel depolarises the membrane, so triggering the adjacent voltage-gated sodium channel and so on. And so the effect travels along the length of the nerve as a wave of depolarisation. Depolarisation is a change in the membrane potential to a less negative value inside.

Neurotransmitter binds to receptor protein (ligand-gated channel) at synapse	Ligand-gated channel opens, so Na$^+$ ions diffuse into neuron	Na$^+$ ion movement causes depolarisation of the plasma membrane	Depolarisation reaches critical threshold level	Voltage-gated channel opens, so Na$^+$ ions diffuse into neuron down electrochemical gradient

How a neurotransmitter triggers a nerve impulse.

Membrane depolarisation leads to a rapid and large change in membrane potential.

Resetting the resting potential

After the wave of depolarisation passes along the neuron, there has to be a process to re-establish the resting potential ready for the next impulse. When the voltage reaches a critically high level, the **voltage-gated Na$^+$ channels** are inactivated (closed) and **voltage-gated K$^+$ channels open**. The K$^+$ ions diffuse out of the neuron, in the opposite direction to the Na$^+$ ions, restoring the resting potential. Once the resting potential is reached, the K$^+$ channel closes again and Na$^+$ channels return to a conformation that allows them to respond again. Through all this, the sodium–potassium pump continues to work and the essential ion gradient is quickly reset, through the active transport of excess ions in and out of the cell.

Voltage-gated channel opens, so Na$^+$ ions diffuse into neuron	Voltage builds up so Na$^+$ channel is inactivated and K$^+$ channel opens	K$^+$ ions diffuse out of the neuron to reverse depolarisation	Resting potential is restored so K$^+$ channels close again and Na$^+$ channels ready again	Sodium-potassium pump resets the electrochemical gradient

How the resting potential is reset.

Setting up the resting potential.
1) Na$^+$/K$^+$ ATPase moves ions.
2) K$^+$ channels allow some leakage.

■ Na$^+$
⬭ K$^+$

Outside
Inside
1
2

DON'T FORGET

Nerve transmission is a wave of depolarisation due to Na$^+$ influx into the neuron.

ONLINE

Find out why nicotine is addictive at www.brightredbooks.net

VIDEO LINK

The processes covered here are much easier to understand if you can see them happening as dynamic processes. Watch the sodium–potassium pump and the nerve impulse at www.brightredbooks.net

① **Resting Potential**
NA⁺/K⁺ pump

② **Depolarisation**
Voltage-gated NA⁺ channel

③ **Repolarisation**
Voltage-gated K⁺ channel

④ **Resting Potential**
NA⁺/K⁺ pump

Nerve impulse transmission.

ONLINE TEST

Head to www.
brightredbooks.net to test
yourself on this topic.

NEUROTRANSMITTERS AND THE SYNAPSE

Neurotransmitters are the means by which nerves communicate across the synapse. The wave of depolarisation cannot spread directly from the membrane of one nerve to the next. Instead, the wave of depolarisation in one cell triggers the release of the **hydrophilic** neurotransmitters at the synapse and these signal molecules trigger the generation of a wave of depolarisation in the receiving cell.

When the wave of depolarisation (action potential) reaches the synapse, **voltage-gated ion channels** open to allow calcium into the cell. This influx encourages the vesicles that the neurotransmitter is stored inside to move along the cytoskeleton and to fuse with the cell membrane. This releases the neurotransmitter, which diffuses across the gap. **Ligand-gated ion channels** are present in the cell membrane of the target cell. When the neurotransmitter binds, the channels change their conformation and this allows sodium ions to enter the cell. If sufficient sodium ions enter, then nearby voltage-gated channels generate a new wave of depolarisation.

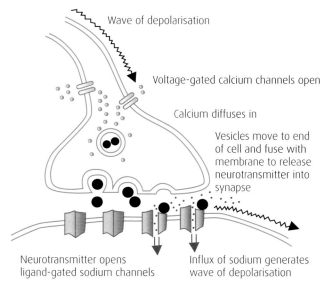

Wave of depolarisation

Voltage-gated calcium channels open

Calcium diffuses in

Vesicles move to end of cell and fuse with membrane to release neurotransmitter into synapse

Neurotransmitter opens ligand-gated sodium channels

Influx of sodium generates wave of depolarisation

A nerve impulse cannot cross a synapse. A signal molecule can, and this transduces the signal as a new nerve impulse.

 THINGS TO DO AND THINK ABOUT

Why does chilli taste 'hot' and mint taste 'cold'?

Heat thermoreceptors have a protein which undergoes a conformational change when temperatures reach 42°C or above. This opens an ion channel, which triggers a nerve impulse. Chillies have capsaicin which binds to this receptor molecule and cause the same conformational change!

Similarly, cold thermoreceptors have proteins which change conformation at 28°C or lower. Menthol binds to these receptors and this is what causes the 'cold' taste of mint!

THE VERTEBRATE EYE

Nerve impulses can be initiated in response to an environmental stimulus. For example, in the vertebrate eye, the retina contains two types of photoreceptor cells, **rods** and **cones**.

Rods function in dim light but do not allow colour perception. Cones are responsible for colour vision and only function in bright light.

DON'T FORGET

Retinal combines with an opsin to form a photoreceptor protein.

RETINAL AND OPSINS

The detection of light by all eukaryotes, from *Euglena* to elephants, uses the light-sensitive molecule called **retinal** to capture the light energy. Retinal is derived from Vitamin A, which itself can be formed from carotene in plants.

Retinal is a **prosthetic group** which is covalently bound to a membrane protein called **opsin**. This retinal–opsin complex is **embedded in membranes** inside **photoreceptor cells**. In rod cells the retinal –opsin complex is called **rhodopsin**.

VIDEO LINK

Watch how activated rhodopsin generates the nerve impulse at www.brightredbooks.net

RHODOPSIN AND THE NERVE IMPULSE

Retinal absorbs a photon of light and rhodopsin changes conformation to photoexcited rhodopsin. Photoexcited rhodopsin triggers a cascade of proteins that will amplify a photon signal and generate a nerve impulse.

The photoexcited rhodopsin activates a G-protein called transducin, which activates the enzyme phosphodiesterase (PDE). A single photoexcited rhodopsin activates hundreds of molecules of G-protein. Each activated G-protein activates one molecule of PDE. PDE catalyses the hydrolysis of a molecule called cyclic GMP (cGMP). Each active PDE molecule breaks down thousands of cGMP molecules per second. The reduction in cGMP concentration, a result of its hydrolysis, affects the function of ion channels in the membrane of rod cells. This results in the closure of ion channels in the membrane of the rod cells, which triggers nerve impulses in neurons in the retina.

The rod cell in darkness has a mechanism that prevents the generation of a nerve impulse. The rhodopsin is inactive and the rod cell produces **cyclic GMP (cGMP)**. This binds to ligand-gated Na$^+$ channels, thus opening the channels so sodium ions leak in across the membrane. The membrane stays depolarised and no nerve impulse is generated.

The rod could be thought of as having a cGMP 'handbrake' – activating the rhodopsin with light removes this handbrake so a nerve impulse can be generated.

The protein cascade (rhodopsin/G-proteins/enzymes/channels) provides a **high degree of amplification**, so stimulation by a single photon results in a large effect on ion movement across the membrane. This gives rod cells **high sensitivity at low light intensities**. Rods can generate a nerve impulse from as few as ten photons of light.

inactive rhodopsin   open Na$^+$ channel

outside

inside   G   cGMP

Na$^+$

Rod cells in darkness.

1. When a photon of light is absorbed by a retinal molecule it causes the **retinal to change shape** which, in turn, causes a **conformational change** in the rhodopsin.

2. The change in the rhodopsin activates **hundreds of G-proteins**, each of which goes on to activate **hundreds of molecules of an enzyme**.

G   enz   enz   enz   cGMP   GMP

3. Each activated enzyme catalyses the **breakdown of cGMP** from many ligand-gated Na$^+$ channels so the **channels close** and inward leakage of sodium ions stops.

4. If there is **sufficient build up of Na$^+$** then the membrane will become **hyperpolarised** and a nerve impulse will be generated.

Na$^+$

Rod cells in light.

PHOTOPSINS AND COLOUR VISION

Cones are less sensitive than rods because they have fewer photoreceptor molecules in their membranes. The photoreceptor molecules generate a nerve impulse in exactly the same way as in rods, but the cones have **photopsins** that are sensitive to different colours. In humans, each cone cell has one of three types of photopsin, each of which has a **maximal sensitivity to a specific wavelength** of light. In humans, one type of photopsin has a maximal sensitivity to blue, one to green and another to red light. Some species in other animal groups (such as insects, fish, reptiles and birds) have photopsins that have a maximal sensitivity to UV light.

Different photopsins are made by **combining retinal with different forms of opsin**. These opsin forms differ by a few amino acids in their primary structures, which means that their tertiary structures are different when they combine with the retinal. This change of structure means that photopsins absorb light across a different range of wavelengths.

Comparing the absorbance spectra of rhodopsin and human photopsins.

ONLINE

Read more about photoreceptor cells at www.brightredbooks.net

DON'T FORGET

Different photopsins in animals have maximal sensitivity to different wavelengths of light (red, green, blue, UV).

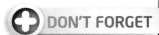
DON'T FORGET

The photon changes the shape of the retinal. The change to the retinal causes the conformational change in the opsin protein.

THINGS TO DO AND THINK ABOUT

The missing part of the **rhodopsin and the nerve impulse** story is the sodium–potassium pumps and permanently open K⁺ channels (see diagram). If you add these to the 'dark' diagram, can you see why the ion concentrations don't build up and the membrane remains depolarised? And if they are added to the 'light' diagram, can you see how the Na⁺ level builds up outside?

ONLINE TEST

Test your knowledge of detecting light at www.brightredbooks.net

REMODELLING THE CYTOSKELETON

STRUCTURE AND FUNCTIONS OF THE CYTOSKELETON

The cytoskeleton is a **network of protein fibres** that extends throughout the cytoplasm in all eukaryotic cells. The cytoskeleton is attached to membrane proteins and gives **mechanical support and shape** to the cell, acting as scaffolding to maintain its shape.

The progressive stages of crenation in a human red blood cell exposed to a hypertonic solution reveal evidence of the internal scaffold of the cytoskeleton.

Organelles are attached to the cytoskeleton and it is involved in the **movement** of cellular components, such as vesicles and chloroplasts. The cytoskeleton is also responsible for the movement of whole cells – pseudopodia, flagella and cilia all rely on cytoskeletal activity.

Three components of the cytoskeleton visualised under fluorescence microscopy. The microtubules are green, the intermediate filaments red and the actin filaments blue. *University of Basel*, imaged by R. Suetterlin, courtesy of C.A. Schoenenberger.

It is possible to view organelles being moved by motor proteins travelling along the cytoskeleton in the laboratory. If a thin pond-plant leaf, such as that of *Elodea*, is viewed under bright field illumination, the chloroplasts are seen to move position. They are being moved by myosin proteins along actin filaments of the cytoskeleton. These are the same proteins that are involved in the contraction of animal muscle tissue.

Microtubules

Microtubules are **hollow cylinders**. They are **polymers** of a dimer made from the soluble globular proteins **α-tubulin** and **β-tubulin**. The dimers are arranged to form microtubules and these have a diameter of 25nm. The length of the microtubules is under the control of the cell through the polymerisation (assembly) or depolymerisation (disassembly) of tubulin at the ends. Microtubules govern the **location and movement** of membrane-bound organelles and other cell components.

Found in all eukaryotic cells, microtubules radiate from the **microtubule-organising centre** (MTOC) or **centrosome**. In animal cells, the centrioles form part of the centrosome and are involved in the organisation of the spindle fibres during cell division.

VIDEO LINK

Head to www.brightredbooks.net to watch a TED talk on this topic and an animation of the cytoskeleton.

A microtubule is a polymer formed from 13 stacks of tubulin dimers.

THE MICROTUBULES AND MITOSIS

Cell division requires the remodelling of the cell's microtubules. The cytoplasmic microtubules are disassembled to form the spindle fibres and the spindle fibres control the **movement of chromosomes** during mitotic and meiotic divisions. The centrosome is duplicated and these then move to opposite ends of the cell. During cell division, the microtubules have three roles:

1. The **aster** or star-shaped tuft of microtubules at each centrosome ensures that the cell division apparatus is correctly located.

2. Some of the **spindle** microtubules consist of microtubules attached to kinetochore proteins at the centromeres of each chromatid.

3. Other microtubules in the spindle do not attach to the chromosomes but instead attach to microtubules from the opposite centrosome.

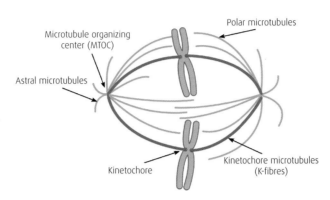

This arrangement allows the separation of the chromatids by the disassembly of the microtubules at the kinetochores, which has the effect of pulling the chromatids to the poles. The rate of assembly and disassembly of microtubules is **far higher** during cell division than at other stages in a cell's life.

During mitosis or meiosis, the microtubules remodel themselves into the spindle. Some microtubules form the aster, which ensures the spindle is correctly aligned within the cell. Some attach to the kinetochore at the centromere and these spindle fibres are responsible for separating the chromatids. Other spindle fibres form the polar microtubules and these help to push the spindle apart during mitosis.

 THINGS TO DO AND THINK ABOUT

Some drugs target microtubule action. Colchicine (from the autumn crocus) binds to soluble tubulin and prevents microtubule reassembly. It is used to induce polyploidy. Paclitaxel (from the yew tree) binds to tubulin in its polymer form and it prevents the disassembly of the microtubules. It is used in chemotherapy as it triggers cell death in cancerous cells with abnormally dynamic microtubule function.

 ONLINE

Read about research into how loss of a dynamic cytoskeleton may be implicated in skin wrinkling and in Alzheimer's disease at www.brightredbooks.net

DON'T FORGET

Microtubules and actin microfilaments are being constantly remodeled by adding monomers at one end and removing them from the other.

 ONLINE TEST

Test yourself on this topic at www.brightredbooks.net

CELL CYCLE

THE SEQUENCE OF EVENTS IN THE CELL CYCLE

Some eukaryotic cells are able to reproduce themselves by following a sequence of events in which their contents are duplicated and divided in two. This **cell cycle** regulates the **growth** and **replacement** of **genetically identical cells** throughout the life of the organism.

The cell cycle consists of interphase and mitosis. The cell contents are built up during **interphase**, which has three phases called G1, S and G2. Interphase is followed by the mitotic (M) phase, which is composed of mitosis (the division of the nucleus) and **cytokinesis** (the division of the cytoplasm to form two cells). So the whole cell cycle is G1 → S → G2 → M.

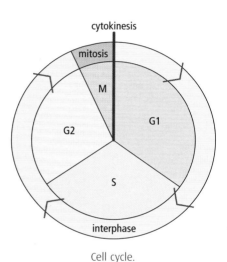

Cell cycle.

Interphase – growth and DNA synthesis

In actively dividing tissue, cells in interphase appear not to be doing anything when viewed by bright field microscopy. However, this is a very **active period** of growth and metabolism; interphase consists of an initial growth phase, G1, followed by an S phase, in which the cell continues to grow and copies its chromosomes, and a further G2 growth phase.

- **G1** is the first **growth stage** – the cell makes new proteins and copies of the organelles.

- **S** phase is when **DNA replication** occurs.

- **G2** is second period of **cell growth** – again, the cell makes more proteins and copies the organelles in preparation for mitosis.

Mitotic phase – mitosis and cytokinesis

In mitosis the chromosomal material is separated by the spindle microtubules. This is followed by cytokinesis, in which the cytoplasm is separated into two daughter cells.

Mitosis is a dynamic continuum of sequential changes described as **prophase, metaphase, anaphase and telophase**. These phases flow from one to the next to divide the nucleus. **Spindle fibres** move the chromosomes during mitosis. These fibres are part of the cytoskeleton (see page 42).

- **Prophase** is the first visible sign of cell division. This is because the DNA **condenses** (coils up) into chromosomes in preparation for being moved. Each chromosome is composed of two sister **chromatids** as DNA replication has already occurred. The cell's microtubules start to disassemble and start to assemble the **spindle fibres and asters** (see page 43) from the MTOC by polymerisation. Some of the spindle fibres attach to the kinetochore proteins at the centromeres of the chromosomes. Tension-sensitive proteins at the kinetochore ensure that one of each chromatid pair is attached to each centrosome. The nuclear membrane breaks down to facilitate the formation of two new nuclei.

- **Metaphase** involves the movement of the chromosomes to line up on the **metaphase plate at the equator** of the spindle. This is an imaginary plane equidistant from the two centrosome poles. The movement is achieved by the polymerisation and depolymerisation of tubulin dimers into the microtubules forming the spindle fibres.

- **Anaphase** is a rapid phase that requires the depolymerisation of the kinetochore end of the spindle fibre. This separates the **sister chromatids**. Once they are separated, the chromatids are called chromosomes in their own right and they are pulled to opposite poles.

- **Telophase** is the phase in which the cell briefly has two nuclei. The separated chromosomes are pulled by the spindle fibres to opposite poles to form **daughter nuclei**. The chromosomes decondense and a nuclear membrane is made again.

contd

Cytokinesis is the division of the cytoplasm to form two **daughter cells**. Different mechanisms are used in animal calls and plant cells. In animal cells, the membrane is pinched in by a circle of actin and myosin fibres; this process is known as cell cleavage. Plant cells have to form a middle lamella and new cell wall between the two daughter cells, and this is done before the membrane is made.

Prophase: the chromosomes (blue in the photo) condense (coil up) and become visible as two joined chromatids. The cell's microtubules (green in the photo) start to form the spindle fibres. The spindle fibres attach to the kinetochores (pink in the photo) at the centromeres of the chromosomes. The nuclear membrane disintegrates.

Metaphase: spindle fibres move the chromosomes, so they line up on the **metaphase plate at the equator** of the spindle.

Anaphase: the spindle fibres separate the **sister chromatids**. Once they are separated, the chromatids are called chromosomes in their own right, and are pulled to the opposite poles.

Telophase: the separated chromosomes form **daughter nuclei**. The chromosomes decondense and a nuclear membrane is made again.

Cytokinesis: the membrane is pulled in by actin and myosin (red in photo) to divide the cytoplasm to form two **daughter cells**. Plant cells have to form a middle lamella and cell wall before the membrane is made.

VIDEO LINK
Visit www.brightredbooks.net and watch a clip to get to grips with the flow of the stages of the cell cycle and mitosis.

DON'T FORGET
When you are asked about the cell cycle, it is important that you know the details of the interphase stages (G1, S and G2), as well as the stages of the mitotic phase.

ONLINE TEST
Head to www.brightredbooks.net to test yourself on this topic.

 THINGS TO DO AND THINK ABOUT

The cell cycle can vary in duration depending on the tissue. A cell in the growing points of a mature plant may stay in G1 for weeks, whereas embryonic sea urchin cells can go through a complete cycle in two hours. When a sample of cells is viewed, the **mitotic index** can be found; this is the **percentage of cells undergoing mitosis** in the sample. If a tissue sample has an unusually high mitotic index, this may indicate a developing tumour.

CONTROL OF THE CELL CYCLE

Cell cycle with checkpoints.

IMPORTANCE OF CELL-CYCLE CONTROL

The cell cycle has many complex events that all have to work perfectly to produce new daughter cells. Those new daughter cells have to be produced at the correct rate and in the correct locations to allow regulated growth and repair.

An **uncontrolled reduction** in the rate of the cell cycle may result in **degenerative disease**. In a degenerative disease, such as Alzheimer's or Parkinson's, insufficient replacement cells are being formed for normal tissue function.

An **uncontrolled increase** in the rate of the cell cycle may result in **tumour formation**. Uncontrolled growth may be benign or may result in a malignant cancer.

A proto-oncogene is a normal gene, usually involved in the control of cell growth or division, which can mutate to form a tumour-promoting oncogene.

CELL-CYCLE CHECKPOINTS

Progression through the cell cycle is regulated by **checkpoints** at G1, G2 and metaphase. Checkpoints are mechanisms within the cell that assess the condition of the cell during the cell cycle and halt progression to the next phase until certain requirements are met.

DNA damage triggers the activation of several proteins, including **p53**.

The **G1 checkpoint** is near the end of G1. Here the **cell size is monitored**. There has to be sufficient cell mass to form two daughter cells. This checkpoint controls entry to the S phase.

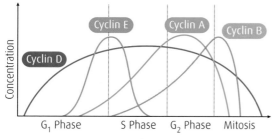

A series of different cyclin proteins are produced during the cell cycle. Each one is able to combine with a cyclin-dependent kinase (CDK) and, once its threshold has been reached, the cell cycle progresses to the next stage of the cell cycle.

If a go-ahead signal is not reached at the G1 checkpoint, the cell may switch to a **non-dividing state** called the **G0 phase**. In the G0 phase, cyclin proteins are not produced, so the cell has left the cell cycle and is said to be 'resting'. The cell will still be active and maybe a fully functioning differentiated cell, but it is no longer concerned with the business of cell division – most of your cells are currently in this 'resting' phase. G0 cells can return to the cell cycle if conditions change.

The **G2 checkpoint** is at the end of G2. This assesses the **success of DNA replication** and any damage to DNA to make sure each daughter cell can receive a complete copy of the DNA. This checkpoint controls entry to mitosis.

The **metaphase checkpoint** is during metaphase. This monitors the **chromosome alignment** to ensure each daughter cell receives one chromatid from each chromosome. This checkpoint controls the progression from metaphase to anaphase. Progression is halted until the chromosomes are aligned correctly on the metaphase plate and attached to the spindle microtubules.

Cyclins

Cyclin proteins accumulate during cell growth and are involved in regulating the cell cycle. As the cell size increases during G1, **cyclin proteins** accumulate, combine with and activate **regulatory proteins** called **cyclin-dependent kinases** (CDKs). The binding of the cyclin to the CDKs, forming what is known as the mitosis-promoting factor, results in the activation of the CDK. **Active CDKs** cause the **phosphorylation** of target proteins that regulate progression through the cell cycle. If a sufficient threshold of phosphorylation is reached, the checkpoint is passed and the cell cycle moves on to the next stage. If an **insufficient threshold** is reached, the cell is held at a checkpoint, as 'stop' is the default setting (except in cancer cells). Without any active CDKs the cell will enter the G0 resting state.

DON'T FORGET

A kinase is an enzyme that phosphorylates a protein substrate.

contd

Retinoblastoma protein

At the G1 checkpoints, **retinoblastoma protein** (Rb) acts as a tumour suppressor by inhibiting the transcription of genes that code for proteins needed for DNA replication. It is a **transcription-factor inhibitor**. These transcription factors are involved in the production of proteins that are required for DNA replication in S phase. With low levels of CDK activity, Rb binds to the **transcription factor E2F**. This **binding of Rb to the transcription factor inhibits the transcription of the genes** required to enter the S phase. Inhibition of the transcription factors is the molecular stop signal of the checkpoint.

If the activity of G1 cyclin-CDK reaches a **sufficient threshold** where each Rb has been repeatedly phosphorylated (14 times), this **phosphorylated Rb** protein can no longer bind to the **transcription factors**, releasing them to promote the transcription of genes required for DNA replication. Cells progress from G1 to the S phase. This phosphorylation of Rb, by preventing its binding to and therefore inhibition of the transcription factors, allows the go-ahead signal to be given at the checkpoint.

Lack of regulation of this CDK–RB–E2F pathway has been detected in almost all malignant cancer cells in humans.

Cyclin level	Absent	Present	Abundant
CDK status	Inactive	Active but in low concentration	Active and in high concentration
Rb protein	Unphosphorylated	Rb with single phosphorylation	Rb with multiple phosphorylation
Transcription factors for DNA replication	Not produced in significant quantity	Transcription inhibited (as TFs present but bound to Rb)	Transcription promoted (as TFs present and not bound to Rb)
Cell-cycle stage	Cell enters G0 (differentiation may be triggered)	G1 checkpoint 'STOP'	G1 → S 'go ahead' at G1 checkpoint

p53 protein

The **p53 protein** is another important part of the G1 checkpoint. It is a **transcription factor** that can stimulate DNA repair, arrest the cell cycle or trigger cell death.

If DNA damage has occurred p53 causes the expression of genes that **stimulate DNA repair** and **arrest the cell cycle**. If the DNA repair is successful, the cell cycle can continue once again.

If the damaged DNA cannot be repaired, then p53 instructs the cell to kill itself through **apoptosis** (see page 48).

The p53 protein has been found to be missing or faulty in about 50% of human cancerous cells – one reason why these cells can divide without being halted at the G1 checkpoint.

 THINGS TO DO AND THINK ABOUT

The genes that are responsible for abnormal cell division are known as proliferation genes and anti-proliferation genes.

Proliferation genes code for proteins that promote cell division, such as CDK genes. Under normal circumstances this would happen only when an external signal is received, for example when a wound needs to be repaired. They are also known as proto-oncogenes because, when they mutate, they form oncogenes, the genes that are found in many cancers. These mutations result in proteins that stimulate excessive cell division and tumour formation, even in the absence of any external signal. Because this mutation only needs to happen in one gene of the pair, oncogenes can be thought of as dominant genes.

Anti-proliferation genes code for proteins that restrict cell division by operating at the cell-cycle checkpoints. Examples would be Rb and p53. Their genes are also known as tumour-suppressor genes because they normally prevent excessive cell division. One functioning gene can still produce the protein to inhibit cell-cycle progression, so both copies of the gene must mutate before control of the cell cycle is lost and a tumour starts to form. For this reason, the cancer-causing mutations of anti-proliferation genes can be thought of as recessive.

 ONLINE

Here's a challenge: head to www.brightredbooks.net and see if you have the know-how to complete the cell cycle

 DON'T FORGET

Remember the exact timings of the checkpoints. The G1 checkpoint is near the end of G1 phase. The G2 checkpoint is at the end of G2 phase. The M checkpoint is during metaphase.

 ONLINE TEST

Test yourself on this topic at www.brightredbooks.net

APOPTOSIS

Most members of the bird order Coraciiformes have syndactylous feet. This means that two of their three forward-pointing toes on each foot are fused together, as can be seen in this grey-headed kingfisher from Tanzania. The cells between the two fused toes (the middle and the outer toe) have not undergone apoptosis during development (unlike the cells between the middle and the inner toe). Kingfishers are sit-and-wait predators and it is thought that the fused toes provide additional stability for long periods spent immobile.

CONTROL OF PROGRAMMED CELL DEATH

In a multicellular organism, growth and development involves not only the careful control of cell division by the cell cycle, but also the careful control of the deliberate destruction of cells by **apoptosis**. For example, in the development of tetrapod limbs, different patterns of programmed cell death result in a different arrangement of fused or free fingers or toes. Apoptosis is also essential during developmental metamorphosis. In mammalian cell cultures, primary cell lines undergo apoptosis after about 60 cell divisions; cancer cell lines that have mutations in their regulation of apoptosis have to be used instead to achieve immortality.

TRIGGERING APOPTOSIS

Programmed cell death (apoptosis) is triggered by **cell-death signals**. These can come from outside of the cell or from within the cell. It is important that the rate of apoptosis is carefully controlled. If the degradation enzymes called **caspases** that achieve apoptosis are overactive, then neurodegenerative diseases can result. On the other hand, underactive caspases can be a cause of tumour development.

The extrinsic pathway (external death signal)

Cell-death signals may originate outwith the cell, for example from a lymphocyte, such as a killer cell that has detected abnormal behaviour of the cell. These **ligands bind** to a surface-receptor protein, causing the receptor protein to **change the conformation** of its subunits on the cytoplasmic side of the membrane. This change acts as a **signal transduction** and triggers a **protein cascade** within the cytoplasm that produces **caspases**.

The intrinsic pathway (internal death signal)

Death signals may also originate within the cell, for example as a result of DNA damage the tumour-suppressor protein of **p53** can also activate a **caspase cascade**. This is achieved through the disruption of the integrity of the mitochondria, which triggers the cascade. Cells may also initiate apoptosis in the absence of cell growth factors.

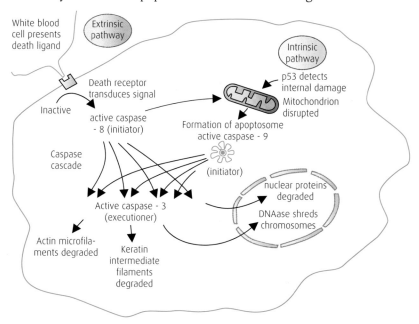

A simplified summary of the cellular pathways that lead to programmed cell death. Note that, whether the starting point was intrinsic or extrinsic, both pathways lead to the same end point. Once the caspase cascade has activated the executioner caspases, the cell's cytoskeleton and nuclear material is shredded.

THE CASPASE CASCADE

The caspase cascade involves a series of **post-translational modifications** to proteins that are already present in the cytoplasm. This allows a **rapid response** to occur, even in circumstances when the cell's nucleus is out of action. The post-translational modifications involve **cleavage** – subunits are removed and they can reassemble to form active caspases. The caspase cascade involves **inactive caspases** becoming **activated**. Each 'initiator' caspase at the beginning of the cascade activates several **executioner caspases**. These act as DNAase, protease and enzymes that destroy the cell. Each executioner caspase degrades over 600 cellular components and this growing cascade destroys the cell.

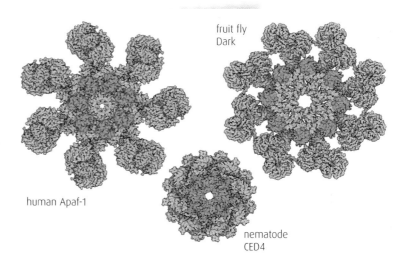

fruit fly
Dark

human Apaf-1

nematode
CED4

The human apoptosome, Apaf-1, is a molecule involved in the cascade that leads to a cell's death. Similar molecules with a similar function are found in other animals. It may be that specific differences in the proteins involved in apoptosis will allow us to develop more targeted drug treatments for tackling parasite infections and their diseases.

FRAGMENTATION OF THE CELL

Once the cellular components have been destroyed, the cell can no longer function. The lack of intact cytoskeleton means that the cell breaks into many small vesicle fragments. These are rapidly engulfed and digested by phagocytic white blood cells.

Time-lapse images showing the *in vitro* apoptosis of a prostate cancer cell treated with the chemotherapy drug *etoposide*. This drug causes DNA damage within the cells, inducing programmed cell death. The fragmentation of the cell is diagnostic of apoptosis and, in a whole organism, allows rapid engulfment by macrophages.

 THINGS TO DO AND THINK ABOUT

The interaction of parasites with apoptosis is worthy of further research. Many parasites induce apoptosis in their host cells as part of their lifecycle. The fever symptoms of malaria are the result of the asexual amplification cycles of *Plasmodium* parasites simultaneously rupturing their host's red blood cells by inducing apoptosis. Other parasites may inhibit apoptosis in their host cell. For example, the endoparasite *Toxoplasma gondii* inhibits the host's intrinsic pathway, preventing apoptosis and providing a longer term niche for parasite survival and asexual reproduction.

However, the fact that parasite cells can also exhibit apoptosis may lead to potential new drug targets. While the apoptotic pathway is relatively well conserved between species, differences may provide the potential for the development of novel drugs; it may be that the problems of resistance to anti-helminth drugs will be sidestepped by drugs designed to induce apoptosis in *Schistosoma*. Even the protozoa, such as *Plasmodium*, have meta-caspases which are sufficiently different from our own caspases to provide good future drug targets.

 ONLINE TEST

Revise this topic by taking the test at www.brightredbooks.net

FIELD TECHNIQUES FOR BIOLOGISTS: HEALTH AND SAFETY

Fieldwork is practical work carried out by a researcher outside of the laboratory or office. As you will have realised already, variables are much harder to control in a natural environment than in a laboratory; this adds additional complexities to the **identification of hazards** and **minimisation of risks** in a field setting. The *Health and Safety at Work Act* requires all hazards and risks to be removed or, where that is not possible, to be reduced as far as is reasonably practicable by control measures. This applies to fieldwork, as much as to any other type of work, and various legislation covers teachers, pupils, students and volunteers engaged in fieldwork.

DON'T FORGET

A hazard is something that can cause harm, whereas a risk is the likelihood of that harm occurring.

DON'T FORGET

The details of this spread will not be assessed in the examination, but you may have to carry out a detailed risk assessment for your Investigation.

HAZARDS ASSOCIATED WITH FIELDWORK

Fieldwork may involve a **wider range of hazards** compared to working in the laboratory. There are three considerations that are particularly relevant when assessing fieldwork for risks:

- terrain
- weather conditions
- isolation
- contact with harmful organisms.

Terrain

Terrain refers to the type of ground where the fieldwork is conducted, and this will dictate the safest type of footwear, and whether harnesses or other safety gear is required. Slipping and tripping are the single most common cause of major injury in UK workplaces, so the hazards associated with uneven ground must be considered. Working outdoors on mountains, near cliffs, in trees, in mud, in water, or on ice pose particular hazards and to minimise their risks appropriate precautions would be taken. For example, without specialist training and equipment to reduce risk of injury, fieldwork in the canopy of tall trees or on cliffs is not possible.

Weather conditions

Even areas with normally innocuous terrain can become hazardous in severe weather. Any fieldwork in the hills of Scotland, for example, requires close consideration of the hazards associated with cold, wet or windy weather. The hazards associated with sun exposure or electrical storms also must be considered. The latter is a good example of a threat that is a low risk but a very high hazard.

Isolation

If the fieldwork site is a long distance from habitation, medical help or transport links, this can pose a hazard. Moving supplies or equipment will be more difficult and evacuation procedures will have to be considered in the event of injury or illness. Hazards and risks associated with lone working also need to be considered.

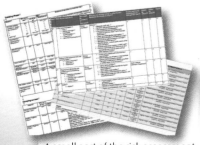

A small part of the risk assessment documentation for a fieldtrip.

RISK ASSESSMENT OF FIELDWORK

Risk assessments should have a level of detail that is appropriate to the types of hazards and the size of the risks. Risk assessments that are cluttered with minor concerns are not helpful as they are less likely to be followed in practice.

contd

ONLINE

To see an example of a Health and Safety policy for university fieldwork, head to www.brightredbooks.net

Even the best risk assessment cannot prevent all incidents. While on a field trip, one of the authors was stung on the head by this box jellyfish. This painful experience was successfully treated with vinegar, which had been included in the medical kit just in case this very unlikely event occurred!

A suitable and sufficient risk assessment

- identifies significant foreseeable hazards associated with the field trip, including travel to and from the location

- evaluates the associated risks (how likely)

- evaluates the severity of the hazards (how harmful)

- identifies appropriate control measures to reduce the level of risk or hazard (control measures can include appropriate equipment, clothing, footwear and means of communication)

- records these safe working practices.

 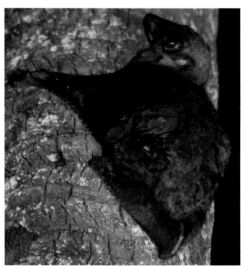

Conducting fieldwork at night requires careful risk assessment. If the risks can be reduced to an acceptable level, it is possible to observe species that are not active during the day, such as the (a) Oriental bay-owl and (b) Malayan colugo, both photographed on a field trip to Tioman in Malaysia. The owl was the first recorded on the island and this sighting added to our understanding of the distribution of this very rarely observed species.

ONLINE TEST

Test yourself on the topic of health and safety at www.brightredbooks.net

THINGS TO DO AND THINK ABOUT

Consider what different hazards and risks you would have to assess before conducting biological fieldwork in an urban city park, versus a small offshore island.

FIELD TECHNIQUES FOR BIOLOGISTS: SAMPLING OF WILD ORGANISMS

Sampling is the gathering of data from part of a population. Sampling can eliminate the need to measure and record every member of a population, as long as the sample selected is representative of the variation in the population being studied (see page 102).

In many studies, the sampling of wild organisms can be achieved through the use of **observations.** In other cases, the organisms have to be **captured** and they may or may not be **released** later, depending on the type of study. Whatever the study design, the sampling must be carried out in a manner that **minimises any impact** on wild species and habitats.

ONLINE

Before sampling wild animals in Scotland, ensure that you have checked the Scottish Natural Heritage website to see whether the species or area is protected. You can find the link at www.brightredbooks.net

The oysterplant, here on a beach in the Northern Isles, has a restricted niche and is rare in Scotland. While there are hundreds of species that are protected in Scotland, surprisingly, this is not one of them. This protected status does differ across the UK, however, so anyone sampling this species would need to be aware of the local differences in legislation.

MINIMISING THE IMPACT OF SAMPLING

In any scientific study, it is important that the measurement method selected does not influence the value of that measurement. In sampling, scientists must consider whether the sample being measured will be affected by the sampling procedure and, if it is, whether that will have any impact on the results being gathered and any potential conclusions being made. If sampling is invasive and involves the temporary or permanent removal of individuals from the population, the benefits of the study must outweigh any negative impact of sampling.

A common lizard in the Cairngorm National Park. The handling of lizards is not recommended, especially by people who are unable to distinguish between the species that have special legal protection and those that do not. In areas that have protected-status designation, such as a National Park, there may be increased protection of particular species or habitats.

In particular, it is essential to consider whether the sampling involves **rare species** or **vulnerable habitats** that are protected by legislation. Rare species are those that are found at low density or those whose total population is small. Vulnerable habitats are those that are easily damaged by human activities. Sampling in either of these cases may be illegal, unless carried out under license.

SAMPLING TECHNIQUES

The chosen technique must be appropriate to the species being sampled.

Point count

A point count is carried out from a selected stationary location and recording all individual organisms observed. It is used for determining species abundance and is a technique that is often used in monitoring bird populations.

Transect

Transects are used for determining changes in community across an environmental gradient, such as a shore. Transects can be in the form of a **line**, which involves a narrow focus of sampling, or a much wider **band**. Whether line or band transects are more applicable depends on the variability of the communities. The

Point counts for endangered water birds in Cambodia. (a) The use of optical aids allows observations to be made without disturbing the birds. (b) Closer approach causes the birds, such as these Oriental darters, to flee and this reduces the accuracy of the sample data gathered.

contd

higher the variability at each point along the transect, the wider the band has to be in order to make the transect representative of the communities being sampled.

Remote detection

In this type of sampling, the monitoring is carried out at distance using sensors, for example by satellite. This is used for global vegetation surveys or for gathering data in areas that are difficult to access.

Quadrats

The use of quadrats ensures that a standard area is being sampled each time a measurement is made. This helps to ensure an equal amount of effort is applied at each sample point, which helps to reduce bias and increase reliability. Quadrats are particularly suitable for sessile (fixed) and slow-moving organisms. The appropriate size of quadrat is determined by how uniformly organisms are distributed in the habitat. Smaller quadrats are suitable when the organisms are small or are very densely packed. The diversity influences the number of samples that will need to be taken – more samples are required with higher diversities. The sample shape is not important, as long as it is uniform and that the area of the quadrat is known.

Students using different sampling strategies in Perthshire. (a) Line transect sampling of the plant communities involved in the succession of a pond. The students are using quadrats systematically every 5 m along the transect to estimate the abundance of each plant species. (b) Comparing the biodiversity of grasslands of different grazing intensities. The students are using random location quadrat sampling within defined areas of each field, which is good practice. However, the choice of quadrat type is poor – can you anticipate what difficulties were encountered through the use of a gridded quadrat?

Capture techniques

The sampling of mobile species may involve capture techniques, such as nets or traps. Birds and bats can be caught in mist nets, but only under license. Night-flying insects can be sampled using a light trap. Small mammals can be caught in Longworth traps. All of these techniques allow the animal in question to be released unharmed.

Elusive species

Some animals are very difficult to sample through normal observation. Instead, camera trapping can be used to provide direct evidence, or scat sampling (counting droppings) can be used to provide indirect evidence.

A sample of blood being taken from a hermit thrush in a study of the metabolism of migrant birds. Mist nets were used to trap a sample of this mobile species. Once the birds were individually ringed, a subsample was selected for the study.

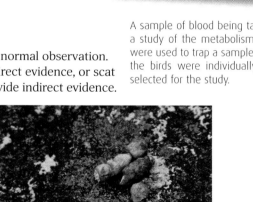

Some animals are elusive and difficult to sample. (a) This leopard in Tanzania was extremely difficult for observers to see, even when it was pointed out by others. (b) The large and obvious Leopard scats, on the other hand, are difficult to miss.

ONLINE TEST

Head to www. brightredbooks.net to test yourself on the sampling of wild organisms.

 THINGS TO DO AND THINK ABOUT

Key legislation that you may need to be aware of before sampling wild organisms in Scotland includes the *Wildlife and Countryside Act 1981*, the *Habitat Regulations 1994* and the *Protection of Badgers Act 1992*.

FIELD TECHNIQUES FOR BIOLOGISTS: IDENTIFICATION

THE CLASSIFICATION OF LIFE

The study of biology is made particularly challenging by the vast diversity of species. As yet there is no real consensus figure for global biodiversity, but it is estimated that 1.5 million species have already been named and described. In addition, estimates suggest that there may be another 10 million species living on the planet. On top of that figure, are the billion species that are likely to have existed on the planet over the last 4.5 billion years that are now extinct.

Of course, these millions of species are all related and are all descended from the last universal ancestor that lived on Earth about 3.5 billion years ago. In this time, mutation, evolution and speciation have resulted in the diversity we see now. To help us understand our observations of an organism (or of its cells, DNA or proteins) it is helpful to **identify** which one of the million living species we are considering. In this way, we are able to collate and compare information gathered about each species. By understanding **taxonomic relationships** between different species, we can make deductions and predictions about how applicable knowledge gained about one species is to another. In this way, the classification of life according to relatedness is central to biological understanding.

DON'T FORGET

It is possible to identify species without understanding taxonomy. It is also possible to have a good idea of the taxonomy of an organism that cannot be specifically identified.

A recent study of the classification of European warblers has led to the recognition of a previously unrecognised species, the Moltoni's warbler. This species breeds in the Mediterranean and spends the winter in Africa, but occasionally overshoots further north in spring. This individual was spotted on Fair Isle and was identified in the field using the tentative information in the latest classification guides. After being trapped for ringing, a biological key was used to confirm the identity. DNA analysis was also used, which supported the identification, and this has been used to help validate the characteristics in the classification guide.

IDENTIFICATION

Identification is the ability to put a species name to a sample. Identification of a sample can be made using classification guides or biological keys, or by analysis of DNA or protein.

contd

Classification guides

tend to focus on one class or order of organisms from one geographical location, such as a guide to the birds of Europe. These guides provide information that allows separation of similar species, such as descriptions of key features, illustrations, habitat preferences, known distributions and seasonal abundance.

More specialist identification information can be found in the form of **biological keys**. These pose a series of questions, often in the form of paired alternative statements, which focus only on the characteristics that allow different species to be separated. In a paired-statement key, each option leads to another paired statement or to the conclusive identification of a species.

The **analysis of DNA or protein** is a powerful technique for the separation of species that are otherwise only subtly different to one another. In addition, it allows the identification of species when only partial or molecular evidence remains.

A classification guide for American warblers.

Section H: Pelvic Fins Thoracic With Less Than Five Soft-rays (continued)

10a *From 7a page 29: dorsal fin with both soft-rays and spines*
Body partly or wholly without scales; no anal spines ....
COTTIDAE Sculpins (Irish lord) Page 118

10b Body scaled; anal fin with spines 11

11a Gill membranes free from isthmus; more spines than soft-rays in dorsal fin except for *Chaenopsis* ....
CLINIDAE Clinids (kelpfish, fringeheads, pikeblenny) Page 173

11b Gill membranes attached to isthmus; more soft-rays than spines in dorsal fin ....
BLENNIIDAE Combtooth blennies Page 172

12a *From 6a page 29: dorsal fin wholly of soft-rays*
Gill membranes joined to isthmus; pelvic fins club-like ....
ZOARCIDAE Eelpouts Page 78

12b Gill membranes free from isthmus (or slightly joined to isthmus in BROTULI-DAE) 13

13a Body oblong; dorsal rays less than 60 ....
ICOSTEIDAE Ragfish Pages 184–185

13b Body elongate; dorsal rays more than 60 .... 14 (anterior rays are spines but appear as soft-rays)

14a Pelvic fin soft-rays not barbel-like, appearing as a small scale or spine; tail forked ....
TRICHIURIDAE Cutlassfishes Page 190

14b Pelvic fin rays as barbel-like structures; caudal fin rounded (if present) 15

15a Pelvic fins attached under shoulder girdle; the two pelvic soft-rays completely joined by a membrane ....
BROTULIDAE Brotulas Pages 72–73

15b Pelvic fins attached under eyes or on chin; the two pelvic soft-rays joined only at base of fin ....
OPHIDIIDAE Cusk-eels Pages 72–73

A biological key for coastal marine fish.

A protein analysis of myoglobins allows species to be identified from small tissue samples.

 THINGS TO DO AND THINK ABOUT

If you need help to identify an organism, there are several great crowd-sourcing websites where expert advice can be sought. One of these is iSPOT, which has a very good track record of providing quick and accurate identifications. Even social media like *Twitter* can be used very effectively with careful choice of hashtags. For example, if it's a moth you would like identified try #teammoth or @MothIDUK.

ONLINE

A link to the fabulous iSPOT can be found at www.brightredbooks.net

 ONLINE TEST

Test yourself on identification at www.brightredbooks.net

FIELD TECHNIQUES FOR BIOLOGISTS: TAXONOMY

ONLINE

Use the link at www. brightredbooks.net to research a range of model organisms.

INTRODUCTION TO TAXONOMY

Taxonomy involves the identification and naming of organisms and their classification into groups based on shared characteristics. Classic taxonomy classification is based on morphology. If the taxonomic groupings are known for a particular organism, scientists can make predictions and inferences about its biology based on what is known about its

The American robin (Turdus migratorius), shown left, can be easily identified by its reddish chest and belly. Taxonomically it is more closely related to the European blackbird than to the superficially similar Eurasian robin (Erathacus rubecula), shown right. The latter individual shown here was photographed in the Canary Islands and may, in fact, be a separate, but closely related, species to the Eurasian robin of Europe – studies of the degree of DNA-sequence divergence have so far proved inconclusive.

relatives. The best-known species within each taxonomic group is considered to be the **model organism** for that group. This is likely to be the species within the group that is the easiest to keep, the easiest to study, the most useful or the most harmful!

DON'T FORGET

You need to know each of these model organisms and the taxonomic group that they belong to.

MODEL ORGANISMS

Model organisms are those that are either easily studied or have been well studied. They may be the best choice of organism for study of a particular biological process (such as cell division). As the members of a taxonomic group are related, the information from the study of a model organism can be applied to other species in that taxonomic group. This is advantageous as those other species may be more difficult to study directly. The following model organisms have been particularly important in the advancement of modern biology.

DON'T FORGET

Model organisms are those species that we know the most about.

Escherichia coli

Escherichia coli is the most-studied member of the bacterial domain. Researchers have been able to culture *E. coli* in laboratories for many years; originally, it was used to study basic bacterial processes and more recently it has been used in biotechnology. For example, the use of restriction enzymes to genetically modify plasmids and transform cells was pioneered using *E. coli*. In addition, the interaction of inducers with repressor proteins in gene expression was first understood using this species.

An *E. coli* of the pathogenic form O157, which is capable of causing severe and sometimes fatal food poisoning. Non-pathogenic forms are common in the human gut. The pathogenic form has additional genes, including those for the shiga toxin protein, probably as a result of transformation by a virus vector.

contd

Arabidopsis thaliana

The flowering plant *Arabidopsis thaliana*, also known as thale cress, is a small rapidly growing plant of the mustard family. It was the first plant to have its entire genome sequenced, and its small genome and small number of chromosomes has made it a good model for the study of genomics, proteomics and metabolomics.

Caenorhabditis elegans

The roundworm, *C. elegans*, is the model organism for the abundant and diverse group that forms the Phylum Nematoda. This species was the first multicellular organism to have its entire genome sequenced. Much of our understanding of developmental biology, apoptosis and meiosis stems from research on this species. Many species of nematodes are parasitic, so research into this species also has the potential for applications in disease control.

A picture of thale cress from an eighteenth-century classification guide. Many mutant varieties were recognised and this led to its use as a model organism.

The developmental pathway of each and every cell in a *C. elegans* roundworm is known and documented. Depending on whether it is a hermaphrodite or a male, a *C. elegans* worm consists of either 959 or 1031 somatic cells; there are no females in this species.

Drosophila melanogaster

The fruit fly is a model arthropod (phylum Arthropoda). Much of the research carried out using *Drosophila* has been related to genetics, mutation and evolution. We share 75% of our genes with the fruit fly and some of their cells have enlarged chromosomes that are very easy to study under the light microscope. This species of fruit fly is very easy to keep in the laboratory, has a short generation time and many different genetic markers that can be easily studied.

ONLINE

Check out the link at www. brightredbooks.net if you want to find out more about *C. elegans*.

Mice, rats and zebrafish

The chordates (phylum Chordata) mice, rats and zebrafish are among the most commonly used model vertebrates for the study of normal and abnormal physiology. Neurological and toxicological studies have been used extensively in all three species.

A transparent embryonic variety of the zebrafish is particularly useful in studies of heart development and function.

ONLINE TEST

Test yourself on taxonomy at www.brightredbooks.net

 THINGS TO DO AND THINK ABOUT

In order to increase the power of the studies in different model organisms, there is now an attempt to ensure that a common language is used across different species to describe the various mutant and wild-type phenotypes. For an example, have a look at the first figure in the PLOS article at www.brightredbooks.net.

FIELD TECHNIQUES FOR BIOLOGISTS: PHYLOGENETICS

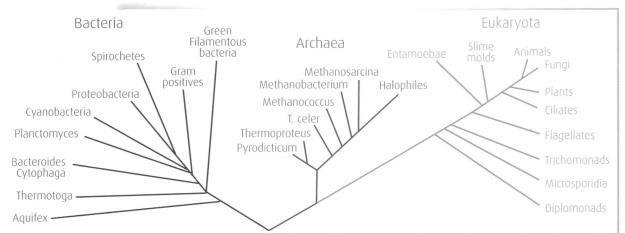

Genome comparison studies have shown life to be divided into three main domains, the Bacteria, the Archaea and the Eukaryota. Note that the Archaea are more closely related to the Eukaryota than they are to the Bacteria.

The molluscs provide an example of divergent evolution – it is not immediately obvious that a snail and an octopus belong in the same phylum.

DON'T FORGET

Molecular sequencing reveals relatedness.

ONLINE

Explore the tree of life online at www.brightredbooks.net

UNDERSTANDING PATTERNS OF EVOLUTION

Phylogenetics is the study of the evolutionary history and relationships among individuals or groups of organisms. Phylogenetics is changing the traditional classification of many organisms. Phylogenetics uses heritable traits such as morphology, DNA sequences and protein structure to make inferences about an organism's evolutionary history and to create a phylogeny (phylogenetic tree) – a diagrammatic hypothesis of relationships. Thousands of phylogenetic studies have now been combined to reveal the overall pattern of evolutionary relationships of the whole tree of life.

Patterns of descent are not always obvious when observing phenotypic characters alone. Evolution can produce closely related species that look very different to one another, and distantly related species that look very similar. The comparison of genetic evidence reveals relatedness that is obscured by this divergent or convergent evolution.

Divergent evolution

Divergent evolution is the development of **differing life forms from a common origin** and it results in closely related forms of life with very different phenotypic characteristics. This occurs when different selection pressures are acting on each lineage. As a result, the ancestral characteristics are lost and are replaced by differing adaptive characteristics in the different lineages. Within the platyhelminths, the body plan of the parasitic tapeworms is quite different from their non-parasitic relatives. In lineages that have few competitors (maybe as a result of a mass extinction event, or in lineages that have had the good fortune to accumulate the mutations necessary for a particularly successful adaptation), divergent evolution can result in a radiation of many forms.

This is a cactus isn't it? Actually, no – it is a Euphorbia from Africa. Cacti are from the Americas but these two families of flowering plants show a strong convergence as a result of exploiting similar niches.

Convergent evolution

Convergent evolution is the **separate evolution of similar phenotypic adaptations** in lineages whose ancestors did not share these adaptations. This occurs when very similar selection pressures are acting on these unrelated lineages. For example, the structure of the eye in ourselves and in the octopus evolved independently in the vertebrates and the cephalopods. Likewise, the parasitic barnacle mentioned on page 81 is a member of one of two lineages of barnacles that have independently converged on this parasitic way of life. Convergent evolution is common; it seems that selection is efficient at arriving at a set of adaptations, even when starting off from different places.

OUR FAMILY TREE

There is now consensus amongst biologists on the relative positions of many phyla in the tree of life. Of course, some areas require more study and taxonomists do not agree on the position of every branch. However, there is overwhelming evidence from molecular sequences, from studies of anatomy, physiology and behaviour, and from fossils, that all life is related and has evolved into the diversity that we see today over the course of billions of years. It is no longer a credible scientific position to doubt this.

Bacteria

There are about 300 000 known types of bacteria. These single-celled organisms are thought to contribute more biomass than all animals and plants put together. We are familiar with bacteria for their key role that they play in nutrient cycles, their importance in modern biotechnology and the various pathogenic types. Examples of the latter include bacteria that cause bubonic plague, leprosy, anthrax, cholera and tuberculosis.

Many bacteria have had their entire genomes sequenced.

Archaea

These are single celled and differ from other forms of life in their ribosomal RNA structure and in the molecular structure of their lipids. The archaea are relatively poorly known – some are extremophiles; others have unusual metabolic activities, such as methanogenesis. There are about 4000 types, many of which are only known from genomic sequences sampled from the environment. There are no known parasitic or pathogenic members of this domain.

Eukaryota

There are over 2 million known species of eukaryotes, which have the shared cellular features of a true nucleus and membrane-covered organelles. The multicellular forms of life are found in this domain, but there are also many single-celled eukaryotes. Within eukaryotes, there are the familiar kingdoms of plants, fungi and animals. Of those three, the plant kingdom is the least closely related. It has major divisions such as mosses, liverworts, ferns, conifers and flowering plants.

Plant division: Moss

Plant division: Liverworts

Plant division: Ferns

Plant division: Conifers

Plant division: Flowering plants

Plant divisions

Animal phylum: Chordata (sea squirts and vertebrates)

Animal phylum: Arththropoda (joint-legged invertebrates: segmented body typically with paired appendages)

Animal phylum: Nematoda (round worms: very diverse, mainly parasitic)

Animal phylum: Platyhelminthes (flatworms: bilateral symmetry, internal organs but no body cavity, many parasitic)

Animal phylum: Mollusca (diverse, many with shells)

Animal phyla

Taxonomic groups

THINGS TO DO AND THINK ABOUT

The comparison of the human genome with other species reveals remarkable similarities. Many gene sequences, such as the *Hox* genes that control developmental segmentation in animals as different as humans and *Drosophila*, have been conserved over long periods of evolutionary change.

ONLINE TEST

Head to www.brightredbooks.net to test yourself on the tree of life.

FIELD TECHNIQUES FOR BIOLOGISTS: MONITORING POPULATIONS

The monitoring of a population involves counting or estimating the number or density of a species on more than one occasion, not simply providing a one-off inventory of the species in an area. Instead, biologists aim to detect changes in populations over time. By doing so, they are more likely to be able to determine the natural phenomena or management actions that are responsible for any changes.

Presence and absence are binary data, with a simple yes or no answer. Abundance has a scale, which may give truly continuous numerical data or which may be expressed in discrete categories such as abundant, common, frequent, occasional and rare.

The proportion of drinking-water tests in Scotland that fail is declining thanks to improvements in sewage-treatment facilities. The most frequent reason for failure is the presence of fecal coliform bacteria in the water. These are an indicator of contamination with pathogens such as *Cryptosporidium*.

INDICATOR SPECIES

Since each species tends to exist only within its particular niche (see page 78), the presence of a species tells us that the environmental conditions in the area meet its fundamental niche conditions. To gain information about a specific environmental condition, such as the presence of specific pollutant, we monitor the **presence, absence** or **abundance** of species that are either **intolerant** (susceptible to) or **tolerant** of (favoured by) that specific environmental condition. You will be familiar with the idea that different forms of lichen have different susceptibilities to sulfur-dioxide pollution. If only the more tolerant forms are found, the area is experiencing relatively high levels of pollution. If the most susceptible forms are present, there must be very little sulfur-dioxide pollution in the local environment.

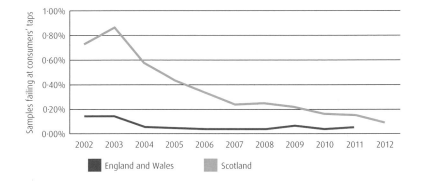

Freshwater sampling for indicators

You may be familiar with the idea of sampling freshwater invertebrates in order to assess river quality. Abundant or increased populations of mayflies indicate unpolluted water that is rich in dissolved oxygen. In contrast, high populations of bloodworms, which are tolerant to low oxygen levels, and absent or reduced populations of the sensitive mayflies indicate that the waterbody is polluted with organic waste.

We sample freshwater supplies to look for indicator species of bacteria. The presence or absence of these coliforms indicates the likelihood of contamination with the Cryptosporidium parasite. This parasite uses the cells lining the small intestine to multiply and this affects the permeability of the gut wall. Cryptosporidiosis is the second biggest cause of diarrhoeal-disease mortality in infants.

contd

Another indicator that is monitored in our rivers, beaches and drinking water supplies is the presence of fecal coliforms; in 2012, for example, over 64 000 fecal coliform tests were carried out on drinking water supplies in Scotland. Fecal coliforms are bacteria such as *E. coli* that originate from mammalian guts, and their presence in a water supply indicates contamination with sewage. More importantly, the presence of fecal coliforms indicates the possibility of the presence of potentially pathogenic organisms such as the human-gut parasite *Cryptosporidium*. Unacceptably high fecal coliform counts result in water from affected treatment works being diverted out of the drinking water supply until successful action has been taken.

This neck-ringed greylag goose was banded in Orkney and then sighted in Lothian. The unique mark allows the movement of this individual between these two sites to be detected. If enough individuals are marked, the movements of the population between breeding and wintering areas can be monitored.

METHODS OF MARKING

When monitoring populations, it is often helpful to be able to identify individual organisms. To do so, various methods of marking have been developed. Methods of marking include banding, tagging, surgical implantation, painting and hair clipping. The method of marking and subsequent observation must minimise the impact on the study species.

Method of marking	Description
Banding	A visible coded metal or plastic loop attached around part of the organism
Tagging	A visible coded metal or plastic tag inserted into or onto the organism
Surgical implantation	A microchip inserted into the organism; read by an electronic reader
Painting	A code painted onto the surface of an organism, such as a shelled mollusc
Hair clipping	A distinctive area of fur trimmed on a small mammal

MARK AND RECAPTURE

Mark and recapture is a method for estimating population size. A sample of the population is captured and marked (M), and released. After an interval of time, a second sample is captured (C). If some of the individuals in this second sample are recaptured (R) then the total population $N = (MC)/R$, assuming that all individuals have an equal chance of capture, that there is no immigration or emigration and that marked and released individuals can mix fully and randomly with the net total population.

 ONLINE

If you see a banded or tagged bird and know what species it is, then you can add to the global pool of scientific knowledge by submitting your sighting online. Find the link at www.brightredbooks.net

Example:

In this example, 26 greylag geese are caught and marked. The size of the population is unknown. Some time later, 21 geese are captured, of which 3 were marked. Work out the size of the total population using the formula $N = (MC)/R$. Once you have done that you could check your answer by counting the entire population.

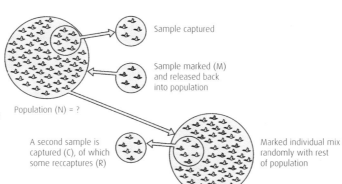

Sample captured

Sample marked (M) and released back into population

Population (N) = ?

A second sample is captured (C), of which some reccaptures (R)

Marked individual mix randomly with rest of population

 ONLINE TEST

Test yourself on monitoring populations at www.brightredbooks.net

 ## THINGS TO DO AND THINK ABOUT

The Comma butterfly is spreading through Scotland at a rate of around 10 miles north per year as a result of climate change. Help to record the spread of this population by submitting any sightings to the iRecord (http://www.brc.ac.uk/irecord/) website.

FIELD TECHNIQUES FOR BIOLOGISTS: MEASURING AND RECORDING ANIMAL BEHAVIOUR

Behaviour is defined as the observable response that an organism makes to an internal or external stimulus.

STUDYING ANIMAL BEHAVIOUR

In school settings, animal-behaviour experiments are often restricted to invertebrate organisms, such as woodlice, and tend to reveal predictable responses to particular stimuli under laboratory conditions. Additionally, attempts are also made to quantify certain aspects of human behaviour, such as in demonstrating learning curves or simple tests of memory or processing speed.

At Advanced Higher level, it is important to recognise that behaviour is an extremely complex adaptation, and that its study involves variables that can be very difficult to identify, measure or control. The inherent variability in many behavioural responses means that **careful experimental design** has to be at the heart of this branch of biology. This variability also means that statistical methods are often used to highlight the significance (or otherwise) of experimental findings.

To help understand complex processes, scientists tend to start off by using a reductionist approach. In behaviour, this means the breaking down of complexity into defined and quantifiable categories. Once lots of conclusions have been drawn about many individual experiments and observations, these can synthesised into a coherent model and we move closer to understanding whole complex system.

Forms of quantitative data

Scientific analysis requires data that have been gathered in a **factual** and **objective** manner. The following measurements are commonly used to quantify animal behaviour:

Some of the most complex behaviours are shown by primates. Here baboons show (a) courtship through meat sharing in yellow baboons, (b) parental care in olive baboons and (c) learning through play in olive baboons.

- **latency** – the interval of time between a stimulus occurring and the response behaviour; for example, the time interval between the appearance of a female stickleback and the male starting his zig-zag dance

- **frequency** – the number of times a behaviour occurs within the observation period; for example the number of zig-zags a male performs in his courtship dance

- **duration** – the length of time each behaviour occurs during the observation period; for example, how long the zig-zag behaviour lasts.

contd

Anthropomorphism

Anthropomorphism is the attribution of human motivation, characteristics or behaviour to non-human animals. The use of anthropomorphism when analysing behaviour should be avoided. For example, it would be an invalid conclusion to assume that a male stickleback is swimming in a zig-zag manner because he is either confused or forgetful. Only through objective study does it become apparent that the zig-zag behaviour is a sign-stimulus to the female to encourage her to follow the male to his nest.

The stickleback provides a classic study of courtship behaviour. Before studying courtship, an ethogram would have been made so that the researchers could be sure their study was repeatable and their findings comparable with those of other studies. In an ethogram, each behaviour is defined clearly.

ETHOGRAMS

An ethogram lists species-specific behaviours to be observed and recorded in the study. Recording the duration of each of the behaviours in the ethogram, together with the total time of observation, allows the proportion of time spent on each behaviour to be calculated in a time budget.

Stickleback courtship: the male is trembling against the female and this stimulates her to lay her eggs in his nest.

An ethogram suitable for the study of stickleback courtship.

Behaviour	Description
Foraging	Searching for food
Feeding	Grabbing food
Cannibalism	Feeding on eggs
Escaping	Rapid swimming ahead of other fish
Courtship: male dance	Swimming in a zig-zag pattern
Courtship: following	Female swimming slowly closely behind male
Courtship: indicating	Male holds body at angle and repeatedly touches nest entrance with mouth
Courtship: entering nest	Female entering nest
Courtship: trembling	Male repeatedly nudging female
Reproduction: egg laying	Female laying eggs
Reproduction: entering nest	Male entering nest
Parental care: nest-building	Male moving weed to nest site
Parental care: guarding	Stationary position in vicinity of nest site
Parental care: fanning	Male fanning nest with fins
Parental care: chasing	Aggression and rapid swimming behind other fish

 VIDEO LINK

Watch the stickleback courtship at www.brightredbooks.net

 DON'T FORGET

An ethnogram is a list of all of the behaviours shown by a species.

THINGS TO DO AND THINK ABOUT

Do you find this image scary or appealing? It may seem strange, but your response to that question could be altered by a parasite, *Toxoplasma*. *Toxoplasma* is a protozoan parasite of cats. As it is a trophic-niche parasite, it returns to its definitive host through the food chain, such as in the body of a rat or a mouse. *Toxoplasma* is known to modify the behaviour of the intermediate host in ways that tend to increase the chances of successful consumption by a feline predator. For example, the degree of fear of and aversion to cats is lowered and infected rodents tend to choose to spend time in areas that have the scent of cat urine. *Toxoplasma* can also infect humans and the effects appear to parallel those in other intermediate hosts – personality traits associated with risk-taking behaviours have been shown to be more common in humans who are infected with the parasite. The mechanisms most probably responsible for these observed changes are an increase in dopamine, increase in testosterone in males and changes to the regulation of key genes in the amygdala, the part of the brain associated with emotional responses. Consider how you would design experiments that could be carried out to investigate the types of changes that occur in infected mice and humans.

 ONLINE TEST

Test yourself on measuring and recording animal behaviour at www.brightredbooks.net

EVOLUTION BY DRIFT AND NATURAL SELECTION

WHAT IS EVOLUTION?

Evolution does not happen to an individual organism in its lifetime. The organism may well change in response to environmental influences, but these changes cannot be passed on to the next generation. For example, bonsai trees are pruned and trained so that they grow small, but the seeds from bonsai trees can still produce full-height offspring.

Evolution happens to a **population** over a number of **generations**. The individuals in the population show genetic variation as they carry different versions of **inherited traits**. Evolution is seen when the **proportions of individuals** with different inherited traits in the population change over a number of generations.

Mutations

Different versions of inherited traits have different DNA base sequences as a result of genetic **mutation**. If a mutation results in a base sequence which codes for a different amino acid in a polypeptide, then the mutation has produced a **novel allele** – a new version of the gene. Other mutations produce new combinations of alleles in the organisms.

There are three possible effects of mutations on the evolutionary fitness of an individual. A large number of mutations are **neutral**, because there is no effect on the evolutionary fitness of the individual. Some mutations are **harmful** because they reduce the individual's fitness. Very rarely, mutations are **beneficial** to the fitness of an individual.

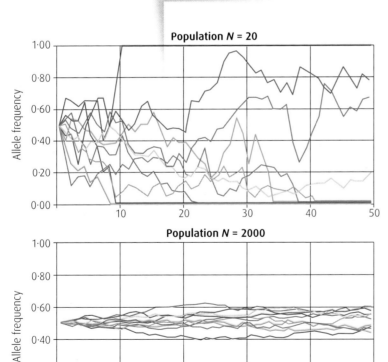

Effect of population size on genetic drift. Each graph shows ten simulations over 50 generations for a hypothetical allele starting at 0·5 frequency.

WHAT CAUSES EVOLUTION?

Evolution occurs through the random process of genetic drift, and the non-random processes of natural selection and sexual selection. All of these mechanisms cause changes to the frequency of inherited traits in a population – the allele frequency – over a number of generations.

Genetic drift

Genetic drift is the **random** increase or decrease in frequency of inherited traits over a number of generations. Genetic drift occurs when chance events cause unpredictable fluctuations in allele frequencies from one generation to the next.

For example **population bottlenecks**, where a population size is reduced dramatically for at least a generation, will cause genetic drift, particularly in alleles not being selected for or against at this time. Also, in **founder effects**, where a few members of the population are isolated from the larger population, the gene pool of the new population is not representative of the original one.

Genetic drift has a greater effect in small populations. Any chance event will randomly affect a sample of the population and a small population is already a small sample. If 25% of a population is randomly selected to pass on

contd

its alleles, then a population of 20 only has 5 breeding individuals, while a population of 2000 still has 500 breeders. This means that alleles are more likely to be lost from the gene pool of a small population. A gene pool is altered by genetic drift because certain alleles may be under-represented or over-represented and allele frequencies change.

Selection results in the non-random increase in the frequency of advantageous alleles and the non-random decrease in the frequency of deleterious alleles.

Natural selection

Natural selection acts on genetic variation in population.

Natural selection is a **non-random** process which selects individuals based on their **survival chances** and thus increases their chances of passing on their inherited traits.

Alleles that are beneficial increase survival, so are more likely to be passed on to the next generation; their frequency will increase. Conversely, alleles which reduce evolutionary fitness reduce survival chances and are less likely to be passed on; they will decrease in frequency in subsequent generations.

Populations produce more offspring than the environment can support. → Individuals with variations that best fit their environment are more likely to survive longer and produce more offspring. → The alleles for the favoured traits are inherited so they are more likely so become more frequent in subsequent generations.

A summary of the process of natural selection.

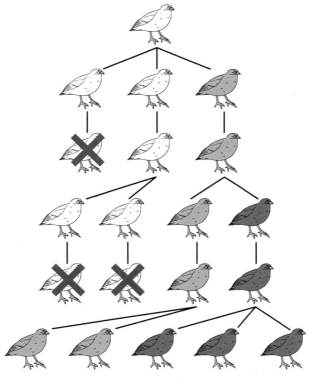

Selection changes the allele frequency in subsequent generations. Here, the allele for darkness could be increasing survival chances of the individuals (natural selection), or increasing their reproductive chances (sexual selection).

DON'T FORGET

Natural selection works on alleles that increase survival chances. Sexual selection works on alleles that increase reproduction chances.

ONLINE

Read some good explanations of the role of chance in drift and selection at www.brightredbooks.net

VIDEO LINK

Watch all the features of natural selection being brilliantly demonstrated in a real population at www.brightredbooks.net

DON'T FORGET

Genetic drift is random. Natural selection and sexual selection are non-random.

VIDEO LINK

Watch an explanation of genetic drift at www.brightredbooks.net

VIDEO LINK

Test yourself on this topic at www.brightredbooks.net

THINGS TO DO AND THINK ABOUT

Changes in the phenotype proportions of a population over generations is not necessarily due to evolution. For example, there has been an increase in the proportion of obese individuals in UK population over last 25 years, but this is not an example of evolution! The population still has the same allele frequency, but the expression of traits has been changed due to environmental changes such as diet and lifestyle.

EVOLUTION BY SEXUAL SELECTION

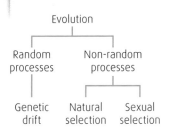

The causes of evolution

SEXUAL SELECTION

Sexual selection is the **non-random** increase in the frequency of alleles that make mating and reproduction more likely. While this sounds similar to natural selection, the selected alleles do not increase survival chances. Some of the sexually selected alleles produce characteristics which may actually decrease the individual's survival chances, e.g. the peacock's long tail. However, if the individual survives, then the characteristic gives it an improved chance of reproducing, so the allele is more likely to be passed on; it will increase in frequency in subsequent generations. Sexual selection may lead to sexual dimorphism.

MALE–MALE RIVALRY

In many sexually dimorphic species, success in competitive male–male rivalry can increase the access of males to females for mating, through conflict (real or ritualised). The successful males will be those that are larger, stronger or have **greater weaponry**, and these are fitness characteristics that will be advantageous to offspring. Males will fight for dominance and access to females, often using elaborate 'weapons' such as antlers, tusks or horns.

(a) The male giraffe is considerably taller than the female and has much bigger horns. The male giraffes exhibit male–male rivalry and fight using their heads and necks for access to females. (b) Two well-matched male impala resort to physical combat.

FEMALE CHOICE

In other species, female choice drives the evolution of conspicuous markings, structures or behaviours in males as females assess the fitness of males.

The male displays tend to reveal '**honest signals**' – characteristics that allow potential mates to assess the genetic quality or fitness of the males. Good phenotypic quality is an indicator of favourable alleles that increase the chances of survival of offspring and low parasite burden, suggesting a healthy individual.

SEXUAL DIMORPHISM

Sexual selection tends to result in distinct differences between the two genders. This sexual dimorphism is defined as **differences in characteristics** between the two sexes of the same species – other than differences in the sex organs. Typically differences are in terms of size and colouration. In most cases of sexual dimorphism, the male is either larger, more heavily armoured, or has more conspicuous markings, structures or behaviour.

contd

Females are generally inconspicuous; males have more conspicuous markings, structures and behaviours.

ONLINE

Watch an example of sexual selection in giant cuttlefish at www.brightredbooks.net

The eider is a sexually dimorphic species that is found around the coasts of Scotland. (a) The male has conspicuous plumage, as well as a noisy courtship display. (b) The female has cryptic camouflage which helps protect the eggs and young during parental care. The young are active soon after hatching and imprint on the female.

REVERSED SEXUAL DIMORPHISM

Some species of birds have reversed sexual dimorphism in which the female is larger or more brightly coloured. In many species of birds of prey, the female is considerably larger than the male – the smaller male is better adapted for hunting small prey that are suitable for feeding his young nestlings during the breeding season. In a couple of species of Arctic wading birds, the females are brighter than the males; the males, as well as the females, incubate clutches of eggs and raise broods of chicks – an adaptation that increases the reproductive fitness of the individuals during the short breeding season.

SELECTION PRESSURES

Selection pressures are the environmental factors that influence which individuals in a population pass on their alleles.

Selection increases the heritability of beneficial traits and reduces the heritability of harmful traits. When **selection pressures** are strong, the rate of evolution will be **more rapid**.

High selection pressures increase the rate of evolution.

Selection pressures can be biotic: competition, predation, disease, parasitism; or abiotic: changes in temperature, light, humidity, pH or salinity.

THINGS TO DO AND THINK ABOUT

The fruit fly *Drosophila melanogaster* is a species that shows some classic features associated with sexual selection such as sexual dimorphism and lekking courtship display.

Males have long been known to wave their wings towards the female during courtship but it was only very recently that biologists recognised the importance of the shimmering colours of the male wings during courtship, particularly when viewed against a dark background.

Drosophila fly

FITNESS AND HARDY-WEINBERG

FITNESS

Fitness is an indication of an individual's ability to be successful at surviving and reproducing. Fitness is a measure of the tendency of some organisms to produce more surviving offspring than competing members of the same species.

Absolute fitness

Absolute fitness is the ratio between the frequency of individuals of a particular genotype after selection and those before selection.

$$Absolute\ fitness = \frac{frequency\ of\ a\ particular\ genotype\ after\ selection}{frequency\ of\ a\ particular\ genotype\ before\ selection}$$

generation

This parent population has 10 individuals and only one has the genotype **dd**. This genotype has a frequency of 0·1 in the parent population. Since this genotype **dd** is found in 2 of the 8 offspring it has a frequency of 0·25 in the next generation. The absolute fitness compares the offspring genotype frequency with the previous generation so, for **dd** it is 0·25 : 0·1 which is 2·5. The absolute fitness of genotype **Dd** is 0·5/0·3, which is 1·7.

Relative fitness

Relative fitness is the ratio of the number of surviving offspring per individual of a particular **genotype** and the number of surviving offspring per individual of the most **successful genotype**.

$$Relative\ fitness = \frac{number\ of\ surviving\ offspring\ per\ individual\ of\ a\ particular\ genotype}{number\ of\ surviving\ offspring\ per\ individual\ of\ the\ most\ successful\ genotype}$$

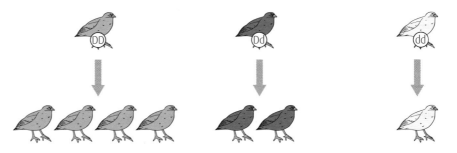

Four surviving offspring   Two surviving offspring   One surviving offspring

The relative fitness is compared to the most successful genotype, DD, with four surviving offspring per individual. Heterozygote, Dd, only had two surviving offspring, so its relative fitness is ²/₄, which is 0.5. dd had only one surviving offspring, so its relative fitness is ¼, which is 0.25.

THE HARDY-WEINBERG PRINCIPLE

The definition of evolution is the change over time in the proportion of individuals in a population differing in one or more inherited traits. The Hardy-Weinberg (HW) principle is the mirror of this idea. It states that, in the **absence of evolutionary influences**, allele and genotype frequencies in a population will **remain constant** over the generations. This stability is called the **Hardy-Weinberg (HW) equilibrium**. The conditions for maintaining the HW equilibrium are:

1. no natural selection – differences in survival chances or reproductive success will alter allele frequencies
2. random mating – if there is inbreeding then random mixing of gametes does not occur, so genotype frequencies will change
3. no mutation – the production of new alleles and the duplication or deletion of existing alleles will alter allele frequencies
4. extremely large population size – smaller populations are more susceptible to the effects of genetic drift altering the allele frequencies
5. no gene flow (through migration, in or out of the population) – the addition or removal of individuals from a population will affect the allele frequency.

Using the HW principle

The HW principle can be used to calculate allele, genotype and phenotype frequencies in a population. The equation for these calculations is shown on the right, where p = frequency of dominant allele and q = frequency of recessive allele.

$$p^2 + 2pq = q^2 = 1$$

To explain this, let's consider a population of 100 cats. At one locus for coat colour, the allele **B** codes for black coat and has an allele frequency of $p = 0.8$, while the allele **b** codes for white coat colour and it has an allele frequency of $q = 0.2$ (the total frequency for both alleles has to add up to 1). We can use these frequencies in a Punnett square to show the probabilities of each allele being inherited in a population: the probability of **B** being inherited is 0·8 while the probability of **b** being inherited is 0·2. We can work out the expected frequencies of the different genotypes in the population by multiplying the probabilities of each genotype receiving their allele combination.

Probability of a gamete with each type of allele

	B ($p = 0.8$)	**b** ($q = 0.2$)
B ($p = 0.8$)	**BB** ($p \times p = 0.8 \times 0.8$) = 0.64	**Bb** ($p \times q = 0.8 \times 0.2$) = 0.16
b ($q = 0.2$)	**Bb** ($p \times q = 0.8 \times 0.2$) = 0.16	**bb** ($q \times q = 0.2 \times 0.2$) = 0.04

Punnett square to work out probabilities of each genotype of offspring in the population

So, the expected frequency of the homozygous dominant genotype **BB** is $p^2 = 0.64$. The expected frequency of the heterozygous genotype **Bb** is $2pq = 0.32$, and the expected frequency of homozygous recessive genotype **bb** is $q^2 = 0.04$.

The HW principle can detect evolution

If the HW equilibrium applies then, if you know the frequency of homozygous recessive individuals in the population, you have q^2 and can find q. And if you have q, then you can find p (since $p + q = 1$). And if you have p and q, then you can work out p^2 and $2pq$ for the frequency of individuals showing the dominant trait. Applying the HW principle to a population can determine whether a **change in allele frequency** is occurring in a population over time. If there are any **changes from the expected genotype frequencies** then this **suggests that evolution is occurring**. In the above example we would expect the population of 100 cats to have 64 + 32 = 96 black cats and 4 white cats. If this is not the case, then at least one of the five conditions for the HW equilibrium must not be operating so the population may be evolving.

 DON'T FORGET

p = frequency of dominant allele, q = frequency of recessive allele.

 VIDEO LINK

A useful video which talks through the Hardy-Weinberg principle and how to use it can be found at www.brightredbooks.net

 VIDEO LINK

Watch the clip at www.brightredbooks.net about how selection increased the frequency of milk tolerance in humans.

 DON'T FORGET

p^2 = frequency of homozygous dominant genotype
$2pq$ = frequency of heterozygous genotype
q^2 = frequency of homozygous recessive genotype

 ONLINE TEST

Test yourself on fitness and the rate of evolution at www.brightredbooks.net

 THINGS TO DO AND THINK ABOUT

In cats, a paler coat colour is caused by being homozygous for the dilution allele **d**. If a population has 25 pale cats out of 100 then you should be able to calculate that the **D** and **d** alleles are equally frequent in the population.

CO-EVOLUTION

CO-EVOLUTION INVOLVES TWO SPECIES

Organisms are exposed to selection pressures and these pressures cause the evolution of the population over generations. If there are two species which have **frequent or close interactions**, they may show co-evolution. Co-evolution is the process by which two or more species evolve in response to selection pressures imposed by each other. This is when a change in the traits of one species acts as a selection pressure on the other species. Co-evolution is frequently seen in pairs of species that have symbiotic interactions.

| 1. Some individuals of Species A have a trait that gives them a selective advantage in their interaction with Species B. | 2. The proportion of individuals of Species A with the beneficial trait increases in the population over generations. | 3. Some individuals of Species B have a trait that now gives them a selective advantage in their interaction with Species A. | 4. The proportion of individuals of Species B with the beneficial trait increases in the population over generations. |

One round of co-evolution. Each round can be started by new traits in either species.

The Red Queen Hypothesis

This hypothesis explains the idea of co-evolution using the analogy of the Red Queen from Lewis Carroll's *Through The Looking Glass*. In this book, the Red Queen runs faster and faster and Alice chases her but, when they stop running, Alice and the Red Queen are still in the same place. The Red Queen Hypothesis states that in a co-evolutionary relationship, change in the traits of one species can act as a selection pressure on the other species.

The body louse has co-evolved with its human host. It lives in clothing and it emerges to feed on the body. The adults die at room temperature, so transmission is by contact between hosts.

SYMBIOTIC INTERACTIONS

Symbiosis is the co-evolved intimate relationship between members of two different species.

The impacts of these relationships can be positive (+), negative (–) or neutral (0) for the individuals involved.

Parasitism, **commensalism** and **mutualism** are types of symbiotic interactions.

Parasitism is a +/– symbiosis

In **parasitic symbiotic** relationships, one species (the **parasite**) benefits in terms of energy or nutrients. The other species (the **host**) is harmed as it loses energy and resources. The parasite uses the host's resources for growth and reproduction; the host, as well as losing resources, also incurs further costs in defending its tissues from parasitic attack.

Adaptation of parasite and host often results in high **host–parasite specificity**. As the symbiosis is the product of co-evolution, a relatively **stable relationship** usually exists between parasites and their hosts. After all, the fittest parasites will be those that maximise their own reproduction and transmission rather than kill their hosts; the fittest hosts will be those that can best tolerate or resist parasitic damage.

Commensalism is a +/0 symbiosis

In **commensal symbiotic** relationships, one species gets a nutritional benefit (the **commensal**) and the other species (the host) is unaffected. A **commensalism** is usually

contd

difficult to establish with certainty, but tends to involve relationships where the commensal utilises either dead parts of the host, the host's waste or takes advantage of a disturbance in the environment caused by the host. One example of a commensal is the remora (or sharkfish) which hitchhikes on the underside of much larger fish hosts.

The remora is thought to benefit as it feeds on the host's faeces; the costs to the host are thought to be negligible – the presence of the remora does not add significantly to the energetic costs of the larger fish.

Mutualism is a +/+ symbiotic relationship

In **mutualistic symbiotic** relationships, **both species** involved in the interaction are interdependent on each other for resources or other services. As both species **benefit**, co-evolution often generates a **structural compatibility** between the mutualistic partners, and an **exchange of metabolic products** between the mutualists often occurs.

Zooxanthellae algae live within the cells of coral polyps: zooxanthellae algae receive carbon dioxide and ammonium from polyp; coral polyp receives sugars from algal photosynthesis.

Three commensal remoras and their host, the endangered shark ray; the remora can cling to the underside of a number of species of larger fish using a sucker-like adaptation on the back of its head.

 DON'T FORGET

Do not confuse the terms symbiosis and mutualism – not all symbioses are beneficial to both partners. Mutualism is always beneficial to both parties

 DON'T FORGET

The ongoing co-evolution of hosts and parasites is a good example of the Red Queen Hypothesis.

 VIDEO LINK

A nice low-tech animation of the Red Queen Hypothesis can be found at www.brightredbooks.net

 ONLINE TEST

Test yourself on this topic at www.brightredbooks.net

 THINGS TO DO AND THINK ABOUT

The human head louse and body louse are subspecies which feed on different parts of the body, and demonstrate resource partitioning. Phylogenetic studies estimate that the body louse diverged from the human head louse about 100 000 years ago, so this hints at the time when our ancestors started to wear some form of clothing.

VARIATION AND SEXUAL REPRODUCTION

DON'T FORGET

It is not strictly true for all sexually reproducing species that only half of the population can produce offspring. In many hermaphroditic species, all individuals can produce offspring.

Why do males exist?

DON'T FORGET

Genetic variation is the essential raw material for natural selection.

COSTS AND BENEFITS OF SEXUAL AND ASEXUAL REPRODUCTION

Evolution favours the individuals that are able to produce the maximum number of surviving offspring using least amount of energy. The simplest way to do this is by using asexual reproduction and it is clear that this evolved long before the more complex cellular processes needed for sexual reproduction. Both forms of reproduction occur today, so how do they compare in their costs?

Costs of asexual reproduction

- Genetic variation of population is low.

Costs of sexual reproduction

- Males are unable to produce offspring. Only half the population – the females – can actually produce offspring.

- Only half of each parent's genome is passed onto offspring, disrupting successful parental genome.

So, since asexual reproduction seems to be the cost effective way to maximise offspring production, why is sexual reproduction the main strategy in virtually all complex organisms? More than 25 different hypotheses have been put forward to try to explain why sexual reproduction is so prevalent. The main stumbling block for them all is in trying to justify the existence of males! The disadvantages of needing males (also listed above) are that it reduces the reproductive effectiveness of the population as a whole, and that it combines the genetic material of two parents to make new offspring, meaning that only **half of each parent's genome** is passed onto offspring, so this **disrupts successful parental genomes**.

Hypotheses suggest that the serious disadvantages of having males are outweighed by the benefits through sexual reproduction of an **increase in genetic variation** in the population. This genetic variation provides the raw material required for adaptation, giving sexually reproducing organisms a better chance of survival under changing selection pressures. The Red Queen hypothesis can explain the persistence of sexual reproduction as the co-evolutionary interactions between parasites and hosts may select for sexually reproducing hosts. Hosts that are better able to resist **and tolerate parasitim** have greater fitness, so this trait increases in the subsequent generations. Parasites are selected to be better able to **feed and reproduce, and to be transmitted to new hosts**. If hosts reproduce sexually, the genetic variability in their offspring reduces the chances that all will be susceptible to infection by parasites.

ASEXUAL REPRODUCTION CAN BE A SUCCESSFUL STRATEGY

Asexual reproduction can be a successful reproductive strategy as whole genomes are passed from parent to offspring. In asexual reproduction, just one parent can produce daughter cells and establish a colony of virtually unlimited size over time. Maintaining the genome of the parent is an advantage, particularly on very narrow, stable niches or when re-colonising disturbed habitats. Asexually reproducing populations are not able to adapt easily to changes in their environment, but mutations can occur that provide some degree of variation and enable some natural selection and evolution to occur. The benefit of asexual reproduction is that offspring can be reproduced more often and in larger numbers than with sexual reproduction.

Asexual reproduction in unicellular organisms

Bacteria, archaea and yeast are unicellular and use asexual reproduction – they simply divide to produce new cells. Many of these organisms also have mechanisms which allow genes to be moved between individuals of the same generation; this is called **horizontal gene transfer**. Examples of these mechanisms include the **plasmids of bacteria and yeast**. These allow the exchange of genetic material and so help to increase the rate of evolution, as is seen in the rapid spread of antibiotic resistance in bacteria.

Vegetative cloning in plants

Eukaryotes principally use sexual reproduction, though many plants can also use asexual reproduction. Flowering plants use their flowers for sexual reproduction but a wide range of methods of **vegetative cloning** has also evolved in flowering plants, including bulbs (daffodils, onion), corms (crocus, gladiolus), tubers (potato, dahlia), stolons (strawberry, spider plants) and rhizomes (ginger, iris). Fungi and non-flowering plants (such as mosses and ferns) use asexually produced spores for dispersal to colonise new habitats.

Garlic cloves are individual bulbs. Each can give rise to a new plant.

Parthenogenesis in animals and lower plants

Asexual reproduction is much less common in animals. A few animal species and lower plants use a process known as **parthenogenesis** (Greek: 'virgin creation') to produce offspring from a female gamete, but without needing males or **fertilisation**. Aphids and stick insects are examples of insects that produce multiple female clones, but can also produce males by deleting a sex chromosome.

Asexual reproduction is extremely rare in vertebrates. Some reptiles like whiptailed lizards and a handful of gecko species exist only as all-female populations that reproduce exclusively by parthenogenesis. These species are all the result of hybridisations between sexual species and they use modified versions of meiosis to produce diploid eggs that develop into female clones.

Female aphid clones.

Parthenogenesis, although rare, is more commonly found in areas with **lower parasitism**. These include **cooler climates** that are disadvantageous to parasites and regions where there is a **low parasite density or diversity**. In these areas the Red Queen's race is being run more slowly, so there is a lower selection pressure on producing offspring with genetic variation.

One species of whiptail lizard, *Cnemidophorus murinus*.

DON'T FORGET

Parasites, and most of their hosts and vectors, are thermoconformers so all will grow and reproduce slower in cooler climates.

CONDITIONS FAVOURING ASEXUAL REPRODUCTION

Using asexual reproduction to produce identical offspring can be beneficial when an organism is well adapted to a **very narrow and stable niche**. For example, aphids use asexual reproduction to quickly exploit the food source provided by new leaf growth, because they have a narrow feeding niche (piercing the phloem of plants) and live in a relatively stable microclimate (amongst plant leaves). Lawns of grass are very stable niches with specific conditions and daisy plants, *Bellis perennis*, use stolons to spread clones across the area. Asexual reproduction is also be useful when **recolonising disturbed habitats**. Buttercup plants, *Ranunculus repens*, use stolons to spread into flower beds with clear soil and gain a competitive advantage by dominating the area before other plants can colonise with seeds.

VIDEO LINK

Find out why aphids use parthenogenesis and then switch to sexual reproduction by watching the clip at www.brightredbooks.net

ONLINE TEST

Test yourself on sexual and asexual reproduction at www.brightredbooks.net

 THINGS TO DO AND THINK ABOUT

The natural variation generated by sexual reproduction has a big influence on experimental design in the life sciences. Biologists have to take account of this variation when sampling a population and analysing the data to make sure that they can distinguish this variation 'noise' from any experimental result or 'signal'.

MEIOSIS PRODUCES HAPLOID CELLS

Organism	Diploid number of chromosomes
Fruit fly, *Drosophila melanogaster*	8
Thale cress, *Arabidopsis thaliana*	10
Round worm, *Caenorhabditis elegans*	12 (hermaphrodites) or 11 (males)
Yeast, *Saccharomyces cerevisiae*	32
Pig, *Sus scrofa*	38
Mouse, *Mus musculus*	40
Rat, *Rattus norvegicus*	42
Zebra fish, *Danio rerio*	54

Diploid numbers of some model organisms used in research.

DON'T FORGET

Sexual reproduction increases variation because it involves crossing over, independent assortment and combining haploid genomes from two individuals.

DON'T FORGET

The diploid or haploid number describes the **number of visible chromosomes**, not the number of copies of genetic information.

Potassium channel

Centromere

Myosin
One chain of collagen
Cyclin dependent kinase

A diagram of the homologous pair of human chromosome 12, which has over 1600 genes. The four genes shown code for proteins that are covered elsewhere in the AH Biology course.

DIPLOID AND HAPLOID

Meiosis is the division of the nucleus that results in the formation of haploid gametes from a diploid gametocyte. The body cells of most eukaryotic organisms have an **even number** of chromosomes because they inherit one set of chromosomes from the female parent and one set from the male parent. All body cells are **diploid** – they have two sets of chromosomes – while gametes carry only one set of chromosomes and are **haploid**. The diploid number for humans is 46, which is two sets of 23 chromosomes.

Homologous chromosomes

The chromosomes in each set have a matching **homologous chromosome** that is the **same size**, has the **same centromere position** and has the **same genes at the same loci** (Latin: 'places', as in 'location'). Though the genes are the same on the homologous chromosomes, the alleles may be different as each chromosome in the pair has been inherited from a different parent.

Sexual reproduction combines haploid genomes

Fertilisation occurs when the haploid nuclei of two gametes fuse together to form a new diploid nucleus. The **combining of haploid genomes** from two different individuals produces a new combination of alleles in the offspring, so variation is increased. The production of haploid gametes starts with a type of cell division called **meiosis**.

MEIOSIS HAS TWO ROUNDS OF CELL DIVISION

Meiotic cell division starts with the interphase stages of the normal cell cycle of a gameteocyte. During the S-phase, the homologous chromosomes replicate. This is still a **diploid cell** with two sets of homologous chromosomes; since each chromosome has been duplicated, it has four sets of genetic information. Meiosis takes this **gamete mother cell** through **two rounds of cell division** which separate the four sets of genetic information and so produce four haploid cells. Some or all of these haploid cells can then become gametes.

Meiosis

Meiosis I has two mechanisms to ensure that the gametes produced by one individual are highly genetically variable: **crossing over** and **independent assortment**. Meiosis II follows the same pattern as mitotic cell division and reduces the quantity of genetic material in the cells.

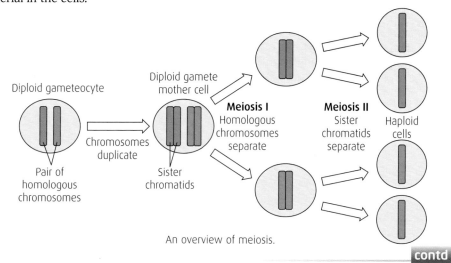

Diploid gameteocyte

Diploid gamete mother cell

Meiosis I
Homologous chromosomes separate

Meiosis II
Sister chromatids separate

Haploid cells

Chromosomes duplicate

Pair of homologous chromosomes

Sister chromatids

An overview of meiosis.

contd

At the start of meiosis I, the chromosomes which have already replicated, condense and become visible. Each chromosome (Greek: 'coloured body') consists of two genetically identical sister chromatids attached at the centromeres. For simplicity, our diagram shows just two homologous pairs.

The homologous chromosomes pair up so that they are aligned, gene by gene, to form a bivalent.

Chiasmata (Greek: 'cross marks') form at random points of contact between non-sister chromatids of a homologous pair and these allow the crossing over and exchange of sections of DNA between homologous chromosomes.

The nuclear membrane breaks down so that microtubules from the centrosomes (see page 45) can connect with the centromeres. The microtubules form spindle fibres linking across the cell and this aligns the homologous chromosomes at the equator, a plane across the middle of the cell. The orientation of the pairs of homologous chromosomes at the equator is random, irrespective of the parental origin of the chromosomes; this is described as independent assortment. For simplicity, our diagram shows the maternal chromosomes (red) at one side and the paternal chromosomes (blue) at the other.

The microtubules of the spindle fibres shorten and the chromosomes of each homologous pair are separated and move towards opposite poles.

A nuclear membrane forms around chromosomes and cytokinesis occurs, forming two daughter cells.

Meiosis I

Meiosis II

sister chromatids

bivalent

chiasmata

centrosome

spindle fibres

At the end of meiosis II, four genetically different haploid cells have been produced.

The new chromosomes group in each end of the cell and a nuclear membrane forms around them; cytokinesis separates the cells.

The microtubules shorten and pull on the centromeres, so the sister chromatids separate to opposite ends of the cell. Immediately after being separated, sister chromatids are called chromosomes (because they can be seen as separate 'coloured bodies').

The nuclear membrane breaks down. Centrosomes again send out microtubules and bind to the centromeres of each sister chromatid. The spindle fibres align the chromosomes across the equators of the cells.

Each cell is haploid, with just one copy of each homologous chromosome (though each cell still has two sets of genetic information). Notice that the sister chromatids are no longer identical, due to the crossing over.

Gamete formation

In human males, meiosis only starts at puberty and all the haploid cells develop into sperm cells.

In human females, it is much more complex. When she is born, each female already has about a million gamete mother cells at the chiasmata stage of meiosis I. After puberty, some of these cells are stimulated to divide further during each menstrual cycle, though only one will reach the chromosome alignment stage of meiosis II before stopping again. The division of meiosis I was asymmetric, so the future ovum is large and the other cell is much smaller. This means that the future ovum has a large amount of cytoplasm to sustain the early embryo, if the ovum is fertilised. The future ovum only completes meiosis II after it has been penetrated by a sperm cell. Again, the division is asymmetric and it is the haploid nucleus of the larger cell that fuses with the sperm nucleus.

THINGS TO DO AND THINK ABOUT

In 2006 a female Komodo dragon at Chester Zoo laid some viable eggs, even though she had never had any contact with a male. This was due to the meiotic haploid cells duplicating to produce diploid cells, which went on to develop. Only the eggs with male embryos hatched – to find out why go to http://www.scientificamerican.com/article/strange-but-true-komodo-d/

VIDEO LINK

Meiosis is a dynamic process so an animation is a good way to really understand what happens. Check out the clip at www.brightredbooks.net

ONLINE

Find out more about the genetic disorders associated with each human chromosome

ONLINE TEST

Head to www.brightredbooks.net and test yourself on this topic.

MEIOSIS AND VARIATION

PRODUCING HAPLOID CELLS WITH VARIATION

Meiosis uses two different processes to produce cells that are genetically variable. Fertilisation then combines the genetic material from two different parents, so the range of possible variation in the offspring is huge.

Independent assortment

When homologous chromosomes are positioned on the equator during meiosis I, there is no control over which chromosome of each pair goes to which side of the cell. They are aligned independently of the other pairs **irrespective of their maternal or paternal origin**. This is called **independent assortment** because each pair is positioned randomly, with no dependence on the way that any other pair has lined up. When these **homologous chromosomes are separated** there are many possible combinations of chromosomes in the resulting haploid cells.

As shown in the diagram, even with just three pairs of homologous chromosomes, there are four possible alignments during meiosis I. When these three homologous pairs are separated by meiosis I and II, this results in $2^3 = 8$ possible combinations of chromosomes in the haploid cells.

The simple process of independent assortment leads to each gamete having a completely random selection of every homologous chromosome, producing **genetic variation** in the gametes. In humans, with 23 pairs, there are $2^{23} = 8\,388\,308$ combinations of chromosomes in the haploid cells.

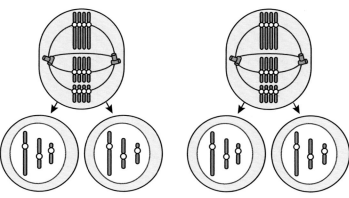

Independent assortment leads to variable gametes.

contd

Crossing over

The chromosomes of multicellular organisms have thousands of genes. For example, *Arabidopsis thaliana* has 25 498 genes on its five chromosomes, and *Drosophila melanogaster* has 15 682 genes on its four chromosomes. From this, it is obvious that many genes must be located on the same chromosome and these are called **linked genes**. If independent assortment was all that happened during meiosis, the chromosomes in the gametes would have exactly the same alleles as the chromosomes that were inherited from the parents. **Chiasmata** allow the chromosomes to exchange sections of DNA with their homologous partner. The homologous chromosomes, therefore, carry some different alleles from each other; the exchange means that chromosomes in the gametes can have **new combinations of alleles** of linked genes. Unsurprisingly, this process is called **recombination**.

This crossing over of DNA is random and produces genetically different recombinant chromosomes.

chiasma

Chiasmata can only form between chromatids of two homologous chromosomes, never between chromatids of the same homologue

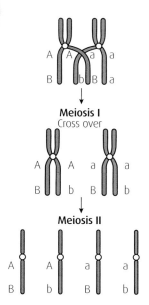

Meiosis I
Cross over

Meiosis II

Crossing over at chiasmata produces recombination of the alleles of linked genes in the gametes. If there was no crossing over, the chromosomes would only have AB or ab as possible allele combinations.

FERTILISATION DURING SEXUAL REPRODUCTION

In summary, there are three processes that help sexually reproducing organisms to produce genetically variable offspring. **Independent assortment** and **crossing over** during meiosis produce variable gametes. **Fertilisation** during sexual reproduction then brings the genetic material from two different parents together in one organism.

Even without crossing over, one pair of human parents could produce over 70 million million possible diploid chromosome combinations. Adding in the effect of crossing over means that the number of different possible allele combination is astronomical. So, except for identical twins, each of us is truly genetically unique in the whole history and future of life on Earth.

THINGS TO DO AND THINK ABOUT

Chiasmata form at **random positions** on the chromosomes. This means that the further apart genes are on a chromosome, the more likely they are to have a chiasma form between them, leading to new allele combinations in the gametes.

Chiasma are more likely between gene A and B than between A and T.

DON'T FORGET

Chiasmata are the structures that allow crossing over. Crossing over produces new combinations of alleles on the chromosomes.

VIDEO LINK

Check out the animation at www.brightredbooks.net which explains the ideas of crossing over and map distance really well.

ONLINE TEST

Test your knowledge of this topic at www.brightredbooks.net

SEX DETERMINATION

We are most familiar with species that have two separate sexes, male and female. The sex of an individual can be determined by **genetic factors** or by **environmental factors**.

There are, however, many species that are **hermaphroditic** which means that each individual has functioning male and female reproductive organs. They produce both male and female gametes and usually have a partner with which to exchange gametes. There are usually mechanisms that mean individuals cannot fertilise themselves. For example, many flowering plants have male stamens and female carpels in the same flower, though they are not usually active at the same time. Land snails are hermaphrodites, so two individuals can entwine their bodies and be fertilised by each other. The benefit to the individual organism is that if the chance of encountering a partner is an uncommon event, there is no requirement for that partner to be of the opposite sex.

SEX CAN BE DETERMINED BY GENETIC FACTORS

Sex chromosomes

Live-bearing mammals, birds and some insects (including *Drosophila*) have sex chromosomes that determine the sex of the individual. These organisms are diploid, so have two full sets of homologous chromosomes. However, one pair of chromosomes is an exception to the normal definition of a homologous pair (see page 68) and these are the **sex chromosomes**, called X and Y in live-bearing mammals. Females have a homologous pair of X chromosomes (XX) while males have one X and a smaller Y chromosome (XY). During meiosis in the male, the X and Y chromosomes pair up because there is a small area of homologous genes near the centromere. Meiosis ensures that there is one sex chromosome in each gamete, so all the gametes from an XX female carry an X chromosome (this the **homogametic** sex). For the XY male, half the gametes carry an X chromosome and the other half carry a Y chromosome (males are the **heterogametic** sex).

Chromosomes from a human female. A male would have X and Y chromosomes.

Sex chromosomes have also evolved in birds and some reptiles. In these animals, the homogametic sex is the male (ZZ) and the heterogametic sex is the female (ZW).

In the live-bearing (most) mammals, it is the **SRY gene on the Y chromosome** which causes the embryo to develop male characteristics. The SRY gene is thought to act as a master switch which triggers a cascade to activate all the male developmental genes in the genome. If there is no SRY gene, then the default pathway causes the embryo to develop as female.

Sex linkage

The X chromosome has many genes which do not have homologous alleles on the smaller Y chromosome and this leads to **sex-linked patterns of inheritance**. Heterogametic males (XY) lack most of the corresponding homologous alleles on the shorter Y. The inheritance of white eyes in Drosophila was the first characteristic in which this sex-linked pattern was worked out. In this case, the dominant allele **R** gives red eyes, while the recessive allele **r** gives white eyes.

In females, a recessive allele **r** on one X chromosome can be masked by a dominant allele **R** on the other X chromosome, giving the red-

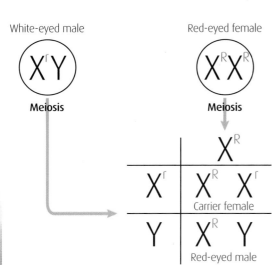

White-eyed male

Red-eyed female

The first sex-linked cross for Drosophila.

contd

eyed phenotype. The heterozygous genotype is shown as X^RX^r and individuals with this genotype are described as **carrier females**. A male with a recessive **r** on the X chromosome will be shown as X^rY and will have the recessive white-eyed phenotype, because the smaller Y chromosome has no homologous gene to mask the effect.

X-chromosome inactivation

Male cells have only one X chromosome and female cells have two. You might think that female cells would produce twice as much of the proteins from the genes on their two X chromosomes, but they don't.

During early embryonic development in homogametic (XX) females, **most of the genes** on one X chromosome in each cell are **inactivated** so the cells have a single working copy of the X chromosome genes. There are a few homologous genes shared by the X and Y chromosomes, so these have to be left active on the inactivated X chromosome. This X-chromosome inactivation is an example of **dosage compensation** which ensures that the females have exactly the same level of gene products as a male and do not get a **double dose of gene products** as this could be harmful to the cells.

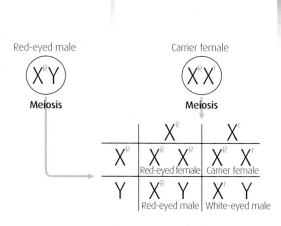

Red-eyed male

Carrier female

Meiosis

Meiosis

	X^R	X^r
X^R	$X^R X^R$ Red-eyed female	$X^R X^r$ Carrier female
Y	X^R Y Red-eyed male	X^r Y White-eyed male

The second sex-linked cross for Drosophila, using the offspring from the first cross.

A tortoiseshell cat has the genotype X^BX^b. Random X-inactivation means that some cells have X^B and show black fur, while other cells have X^b and show ginger fur.

The phenotype of a male always shows the effect of the genes that are inherited on the X chromosome. Females who inherit a deleterious allele (whether dominant or recessive) on one of their X chromosomes are less likely to be affected by its effects. Because X-chromosome **inactivation is random** about half of the cells in any tissue will have a working copy of the gene.

DON'T FORGET

Sex linkage is due to genes on the X chromosome.

DON'T FORGET

Either X chromosome can be inactivated in a cell – inactivation is random.

ONLINE

Find out more about sex linkage at www.brightredbooks.net

VIDEO LINK

An explanation of the sex-linked inheritance of haemophilia in humans can be seen at www.brightredbooks.net

ONLINE TEST

Revise this topic by taking the test at www.brightredbooks.net

SEX AND SEX RATIO CAN BE DETERMINED BY ENVIRONMENTAL FACTORS

For some species, there are environmental factors which can change the sex of embryos or adults. For example, in reptiles, environmental sex determination is controlled by environmental temperature of egg incubation. In others, the sex ratio of the offspring produced by the parents can be adjusted in response to resource availability.

Environmental factor	Example	Effect on sex, or sex ratio
Temperature	Hermann's tortoise	Incubation of eggs at less than 31°C produces all male offspring and above 32°C gives all females.
Size	Clown fish	These live in groups with one large female and some smaller females. When the large female is removed, the largest male becomes a female.
Competition	Lesser mouse lemur	If a solitary female detects urine of another female, she produces more male offspring.
Parasitic infection	Insects infected by *Wolbachia* bacteria	Bacterial infection of the eggs kills the males or feminises them.

THINGS TO DO AND THINK ABOUT

Occasionally a gamete carries two X chromosomes instead of just one, due to spindle failure during meiosis. This leads to offspring with an extra sex chromosome, so they could be XXX or XXY. A person with XXX will develop as a female and will have two of her X chromosomes inactivated. A person with XXY will develop as a male because of the SRY gene, and they will have one inactivated X chromosome.

PARENTAL INVESTMENT

Parental investment can include parental care. (a) Mammals invest in parental care – this vervet monkey mother is providing resources directly from her body when suckling a youngster. (b) Parental care also involves the protection of young. Here a black-naped tern attacks a white-bellied sea-eagle many times its own size – a risk it will only take in the protection of its young.

INTRODUCTION

Parental investment is the use of resources by a parent to benefit future or existing offspring. Investing resources in offspring is obviously **costly** to the parent. The **benefits** are that it can result in increased numbers of offspring and their improved chance of survival, thereby increasing the evolutionary fitness of the parent.

Parental investment can be in terms of resources used in the production of gametes, resources used to provide an environment that is suitable for fertilisation or resources used in parental care – the protection and nurture of any offspring produced. Organisms may invest in offspring that have already been produced or offspring that may be produced in the future.

COMPARISON OF SPERM AND EGG PRODUCTION

Parental investment begins with the production of gametes. There is an inequality in the investment required in the production of individual eggs and sperm cells. There is a selection pressure favouring larger eggs, as these will contain an energy store for new offspring. At the same time the sperm have to be fast moving in order to reach an egg rapidly, so there is a selection pressure for them to contain no excess mass.

In humans, females have about 2 million egg follicles, but invest only in about 450 of these; just 1 or 2 are ovulated at any one time. In contrast, males produce about 500 billion mature sperm in a lifetime, of which around 500 million can be ejaculated at one time. There is greater investment by females in individual egg structures, and, in mammals, also in the uterus and during gestation.

Comparison of fertilisation strategies.

Type of fertilisation	Description	Costs	Benefits	Note
External	Gametes are released directly into the environment.	Chances of fertilisation are lower, so many gametes are required. No opportunity for parental care. Few offspring survive.	No increased exposure to predation or parasites. Very large numbers of offspring can be produced.	Many mobile organisms that use external fertilisation only release gametes when in close contact with a potential mate.
Internal	Gametes are released into the reproductive tract of the female.	Finding a mate requires energy expenditure and direct transfer of gametes from one partner to another.	Fewer eggs need to be released as chances of fertilisation are higher. Offspring can be retained internally. Higher offspring survival.	A general trend is that more sperm is produced in species where there is more competition for fertilisation.

There is far greater parental investment involved in the production of an egg by a female than in a sperm by a male parent.

The difference in size between the sperm and the egg is shown clearly in the picture of mammalian fertilisation. The egg is estimated to have 100 000 times the volume of the sperm and is, therefore, a much more costly cell to produce.

R-SELECTED AND K-SELECTED ORGANISMS

This simplistic classification is based on level of parental investment in offspring and number of offspring produced. Those that are said to be **r-selected** tend to be small species that produce many offspring, each of which has a low chance of survival. Characteristics of r-selected species: smaller; shorter generation time; reproduce early, often only once; produce many small offspring each of which receives low energy input and limited parental care; most offspring do not reach adulthood. This is a successful evolutionary strategy for opportunistic species in unstable environments. **K-selected** species tend to be longer-lived and are more likely to be subject to strong intra-specific competition for resources in stable environments. Characteristics of K-selected species: large; long-lived; slow to mature; can reproduce many times in lifetime; produce few larger offspring, each with a high level of parental care; many offspring have high probability of surviving to adulthood.

 VIDEO LINK

Watch synchronised spawning of a mobile externally fertilised species, the horseshoe crab at www.brightredbooks.net

 ONLINE TEST

Test your knowledge of this topic at www.brightredbooks.net

The African elephant is a classic example of a K-selected species. The gestation period is two years and there is an extended period of parental care, as shown here.

 ## THINGS TO DO AND THINK ABOUT

The bee orchid is a sessile organism that manipulates a drone bee (male) into moving its pollen from flower to flower to achieve pollination. The flower (pictured here) mimics the sign stimulus of the queen bee and the drones are duped into mating with them. Mating with a series of bee-orchid flowers is of no benefit to the drone, but is of great benefit to the plant. More normally, the co-evolution of pollination is mutualistic and the insects are 'paid' by plants with nectar for their pollination duties.

REPRODUCTIVE BEHAVIOURS AND MATING SYSTEMS IN ANIMALS

MATING SYSTEMS

Mating systems are based on how many mates an individual has during one breeding season.

In **polygamy** individuals of one sex have more than one mate. Lekking (see page 83) species are a good example of polygamy. In **polygyny**, one male mates exclusively with a group of females. In **polyandry**, one female mates with a number of males in the same breeding season.

In **monogamy**, each individual only shares gametes with one other individual to the exclusion of all others. DNA fingerprinting studies have revealed that many species that were thought to be monogamous actually have a proportion of extra-pair copulations. The *Schistosoma* parasite is extremely monogamous – the female of the pair lives within a canal-like structure in the body of the male.

The female of the monogamous *Schistosoma mansoni* parasite lives in a groove in the body of the male. The male is larger with a roughened surface. The female is narrower and has a smooth surface.

ONLINE TEST ✓

Watch the stickleback courtship at www. brightredbooks.net

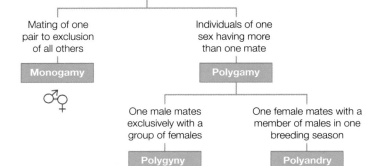

Mating systems

Mating of one pair to exclusion of all others → **Monogamy**

Individuals of one sex having more than one mate → **Polygamy**

One male mates exclusively with a group of females → **Polygyny**

One female mates with a member of males in one breeding season → **Polyandry**

COURTSHIP AND FIXED-ACTION PATTERNS

Courtship involves behaviours and characteristics associated with mate selection. DNA sequences that result in higher chances of successful breeding are favoured by sexual selection. The phenotypes associated with these sequences are not the same ones that would be selected by natural selection alone – they may not improve an individual's chances of survival. However, an increased chance of successful reproduction can lead to an overall increase in evolutionary fitness. As a result, sexual selection results in the evolution of elaborate and intricate courtship displays and sexual dimorphism.

Many birds and fish show ritualised courtship behaviours in which a specific **sign stimulus** from one individual produces a specific **fixed-action pattern response** in the other. This type of response is instinctive and thought to vary little between members of the same species. For example, in the courtship of stickleback, the swollen belly of a female fish acts a sign stimulus to for the male to commence his zig-zag courtship dance. If uninterrupted, a series of sign stimuli and fixed-action pattern responses lead the stickleback pair through the complete courtship to the successful fertilisation of eggs (see also page 59).

IMPRINTING AND COURTSHIP

Mate choice can be influenced by sexual imprinting early in life. Imprinting is an **irreversible** developmental process that occurs during a **critical time period** in young animals. Imprinting increases fitness through natural selection, as forming an attachment to a parent that is providing care increases survival chances. In addition, imprinting can **influence mate choice** later in life as offspring may select mates that resemble parental phenotypes.

The herring gull (left) and lesser black-backed gull (right) are two distinct species that are commonly seen in school grounds. Very rarely, these species interbreed to produce hybrid offspring (centre). The incidence of mixed pairs has been shown to be greatly increased among birds raised by parents of the wrong species as a result of cross-fostering experiments.

LEKKING

Lekking involves **communal displaying** by groups of males. Females visit the lek area to assess males and select a suitable mate. In lekking species, there can be **alternative successful strategies** for males: dominant males tend to be larger and occupy the centre of the lek. Subordinate and juveniles are at the fringes as satellite males attempting to intercept females at the periphery of the lek area.

The black grouse is a lekking species found in Scotland. The display reveals the physical fitness, genetic quality and parasite burden of the male (right) as the female assesses the redness of his eye wattle, the cleanliness of his white undertail feathers, the symmetry of the plumage and the intensity of his leaping and calling. During the display, female choice occurs.

ONLINE

Watch the incredible display of birds of paradise at www.brightredbooks.net

ONLINE

Check out this mind-boggling lekking display of the sage grouse at www.brightredbooks.net

ONLINE TEST

Test your knowledge of courtship at www.brightredbooks.net

THINGS TO DO AND THINK ABOUT

In one lekking species, the ruff, there are three distinct types of male. **Territorial males** are larger than females and have a dark ruff of feathers around the neck. Territorial males fight each other for the best positions in the lek. **Satellite males** are slightly smaller, less intensely coloured and are tolerated at low density by territorial males as having a larger number of males at a lek is advantageous (it attracts more females). **Sneaker males** are the same size and plumage as females. Genetic studies have shown that each type of male is the result of a 4 million year old chromosomal inversion mutation that affects 90 genes, including those for pigmentation and testosterone metabolism. Crossing over cannot occur at inversions in heterozygous individuals, so the 90 genes are passed on together as a single 'supergene'.

THE PARASITE NICHE

VIDEO LINK

Watch about resource partitioning at www. brightredbooks.net

DON'T FORGET

The fundamental niche is the *theoretical* niche, whereas the realised niche is the *reality*.

ECOLOGICAL NICHE

The concept of the **ecological niche** attempts to summarise all those factors that influence the distribution of an individual species. At its simplest level, niche was originally defined as the role an organism plays in the living community – such as 'woodland herbivore' or 'grassland carnivore'. Clearly no herbivore could survive in all types of woodland, so a more sophisticated definition of niche is required.

The concept of the ecological niche must include many factors (or dimensions). The dimensions that have to be considered include **abiotic factors** (e.g. temperature, humidity, soil pH, salinity, light intensity, pollution, gas concentrations, minerals) as well as **biotic interactions** within the community (e.g. predator–prey interactions, competition, parasitism). The ecological niche is, therefore, best defined as the **multidimensional summary of tolerances and requirements of a species**.

Fundamental and realised niches

- The **fundamental niche** of a species is the set of resources that it is capable of using in the absence of any interspecific competition (competition with other species).

- The **realised niche** is the set of resources that the species *actually* uses in response to the presence of interspecific competition.

The difference between the fundamental niche and realised niche of a species.

Competitive-exclusion principle

In some cases of interspecific competition, the realised niches of the two species may be extremely similar. One species will lose out more in the competition and so its population will decline, leading to **local extinction**. This observation is known as the **competitive-exclusion principle**. For example, grey squirrels, which were introduced into the UK, are able to eat seeds from deciduous trees before they are fully ripe and so are able to out-compete red squirrels in these habitats.

VIDEO LINK

Check out the cartoon-style explanation of host types at www.brightredbooks.net

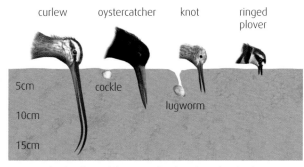

The beaks and foraging depths of wading birds.

Resource partitioning

Where two species living in a habitat have similar requirements, it may be that the realised niches are sufficiently different for them to co-exist. In this case, **resource partitioning** can occur whereby the two species exploit different components of the resource, thus reducing potential competition. The evolution of different beak lengths and foraging behaviours in waders has allowed various species to exploit food of different types and at different depths in their shared habitat.

THE NICHE OF PARASITES

Symbiosis ('together living') refers to intimate associations between individual organisms of different species. Parasitism is a symbiotic interaction between a parasite and its host (+/−). Parasites gain benefit in terms of nutrients at the expense of the host. The parasite uses the host's resources for growth and reproduction; the host, as well as losing resources, also incurs further costs in defending its tissues from parasitic attack. **Ectoparasites** live and feed on the surface of their host, e.g. ticks, lice, fleas. **Endoparasites** live within the host, e.g. tapeworm, *Plasmodium* (causes malaria), rhinovirus (causes common cold).

contd

In a predator–prey relationship, the predator and the prey have similar reproductive potential, e.g. cats and mice can both produce tens of offspring each year. In a parasitic relationship, the reproductive potential of the parasite is much greater than that of the host, e.g. a cat flea can produce thousands of offspring in a year.

Human crab louse – an ectoparasite which is highly specific to the pubic hair of humans.

ONLINE

Find out more about the three types of human louse at www.brightredbooks.net

Co-evolution and the parasite niche

According to the Red Queen Hypothesis, parasite adaptations have been selected in response to the particular adaptations that have evolved in the host species. Because of this, parasites tend to have a **narrow specialised niche**: this is true both in terms of being **host-specific** and also very specific in their ways of exploiting that host. For example, there are three ectoparasitic species of louse which are only found on humans, and each louse species has a restricted area of the body on which they feed – an example of resource partitioning.

Many of a parasite's needs are provided by the host, so this means that parasites have become **degenerate** – they lack structures and organs that are found in other organisms. For example, the tapeworm is an endoparasite that lives in the small intestine of its host and is surrounded by digested food, so it has no need for a digestive system. The production of unused tissue in an organism is a waste of resources, so evolution has favoured the loss of these tissues.

Parasite-lifecycle definitions

Some parasites require only one host to complete their life cycle. Many parasitic lifecycles can involve more than one species. The **definitive host** is the organism on which or in which the parasite reaches sexual maturity and so carries out sexual reproduction. An **intermediate host** is one in which developmental stages happen to complete the parasite's lifecycle. For example, the pork tapeworm reproduces sexually in the gut cavity of humans (the definitive host). The tapeworm sheds eggs into the gut cavity and these eggs pass out in faeces. The eggs are eaten by pigs (the intermediate host) where they hatch and develop as slowly in sacs called cysts in the muscle tissue before being consumed by humans.

Parasite lifecycles may also have species that play an **active part** in the transmission of the parasite. These are called **vectors** and they may also be hosts. For example, the mosquito is the vector for the malarial parasite, and it is also the definitive host. But vectors are not always hosts; aphids are vectors for plant viruses, but the viruses have no lifecycle stages in the aphids.

DON'T FORGET

The terms *definitive host* and *intermediate host* describe different aspects of a parasite lifecycle, and either of these host types could also be a *vector*.

THINGS TO DO AND THINK ABOUT

Many parasites carry out asexual reproduction in the intermediate hosts; why would this be a benefit to the parasite?

The population of the parasite is rapidly built up by asexual reproduction so there are many more parasites present to increase the chance of dispersing to a new definitive host.

ONLINE TEST

Head to www.brightredbooks.net to test yourself on the parasite niche.

PARASITIC LIFECYCLES

PLASMODIUM AND SCHISTOSOMA PARASITES

Two key examples of parasites that need intermediate hosts to complete the development of their lifecycle are noted below and in the diagrams:

1. *Schistosoma* are platyhelminths which cause the disease schistosomiasis in humans. This parasite needs to spend part of its lifecycle in a snail, so that it can develop into a larval form which can penetrate the skin of a human, its definitive host.

2. *Plasmodium* are protists which cause the malaria disease in humans. The parasites have to spend part of the lifecycle in humans so that they can develop into male and female forms ready to infect a mosquito, its definitive host.

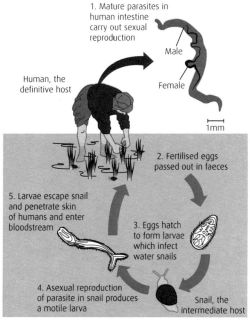

The lifecycle of *Schistosoma* parasites.

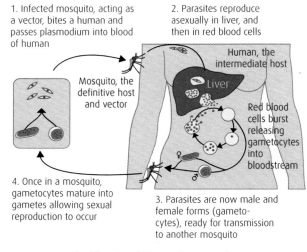

The lifecycle of *Plasmodium* parasites.

ONLINE

How does malaria affect humans? Find out at www.brightredbooks.net

DON'T FORGET

The definitive host is the one in which the parasite reproduces sexually.

VIDEO LINK

Watch the life of the malarial parasite at www.brightredbooks.net

THE 'LIFE' OF A VIRUS

Viruses are infectious parasitic agents that can only replicate inside a host cell. They don't quite meet most biologists' definition of 'living'. The viruses can't carry out any of the normal functions for life except for one – reproduction, and they can only do this in the cell of a living organism.

Virus structure

For reproduction to occur, viruses have to contain genetic information stored in a **nucleic acid** (DNA or RNA). This nucleic acid is packaged inside a **protective protein coat** (the capsid) and some viruses are also surrounded by a phospholipid membrane derived from host cell materials. The outer surface of a virus has proteins that are coded for by the viral genes. These proteins are called **antigens**, because a cell from the host organism may or may not be able to detect them as foreign and initiate an immune response.

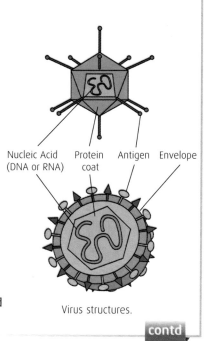

Virus structures.

contd

Virus reproduction

DNA viruses have their genetic material in the form of DNA and these include smallpox, herpes, and chickenpox viruses. These viruses reproduce using the steps shown in the diagram.

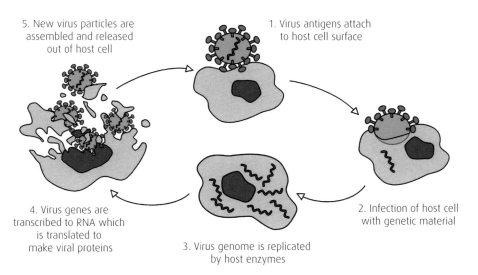

5. New virus particles are assembled and released out of host cell

1. Virus antigens attach to host cell surface

4. Virus genes are transcribed to RNA which is translated to make viral proteins

3. Virus genome is replicated by host enzymes

2. Infection of host cell with genetic material

How DNA viruses reproduce.

RNA viruses (such as influenza, Ebola, hepatitis C, polio, rabies and measles) have an RNA genome. These viruses use the same process of reproduction as the DNA viruses except, at Step 3, the viral RNA genome is replicated directly using an enzyme from the virus. Viral DNA is never made.

RNA retroviruses, such as HIV, use a slightly more complex process for reproduction, though it is really just Step 3 that is different. These viruses use the enzyme **reverse transcriptase** to form a DNA copy of the virus genome. This DNA is then inserted into the genome of the host cell. The virus genome can then be replicated as part of the normal cell cycle, so the virus genome will always be in the host cells. Viral genes can then be expressed to form new viral particles.

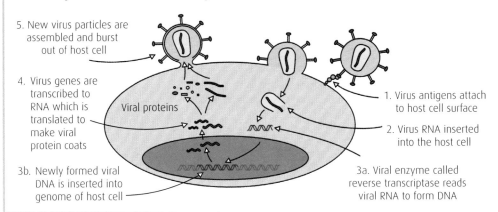

5. New virus particles are assembled and burst out of host cell

4. Virus genes are transcribed to RNA which is translated to make viral protein coats

Viral proteins

3b. Newly formed viral DNA is inserted into genome of host cell

1. Virus antigens attach to host cell surface

2. Virus RNA inserted into the host cell

3a. Viral enzyme called reverse transcriptase reads viral RNA to form DNA

THINGS TO DO AND THINK ABOUT

The treatment of HIV infection has become very effective at preventing the development of AIDS in the patient. The treatment uses a combination of three or more antiretroviral drugs to stop the virus replicating. The combination of drugs is needed because a single antiretroviral drug is a simple selection pressure, so the virus can quickly evolve and become resistant to that drug.

VIDEO LINK

Watch the lifecycle of one species of *Schistosoma* at www.brightredbooks.net

DON'T FORGET

Most RNA viruses simply replicate their RNA so they are not retroviruses.

DON'T FORGET

Reproduction of DNA viruses, RNA viruses and RNA retroviruses only differs fundamentally in the middle steps.

DON'T FORGET

The genetic material of viruses can be DNA or RNA.

VIDEO LINK

Watch the story of retroviral reproduction at www.brightredbooks.net

ONLINE TEST

Head to www.brightredbooks.net to test yourself on parasitic lifecycles.

TRANSMISSION AND VIRULENCE

The spread of a parasite to a new host is called **transmission**. The harm that a parasite causes to a host species is called **virulence**. This reduces the host's evolutionary fitness because the parasite is redirecting the host's resources to parasite reproduction.

Human head louse, showing human blood in the digestive system and hook-like claws to hold on to fine human hair.

VIDEO LINK

Check out the TED-Ed Lesson with some examples of host behaviour that is modified by parasites at www.brightredbooks.net

DON'T FORGET

You don't need to learn the specific examples of these extended phenotypes, just the five key categories.

ONLINE

Learn more about mud-snail gigantism at www.brightredbooks.net

ONLINE

Read the *Sacculina* horror story at www.brightredbooks.net

FACTORS THAT INCREASE TRANSMISSION RATES

If a population of hosts is **overcrowded** and living at **high density** in a habitat, then parasites are able to pass more easily to a new host. This is important for parasites that are transmitted by direct contact and so tend to have a low transmission rate. For example, the human head louse is more rapidly spread when people have their heads close together, such as in schools...

The use of **vectors** has evolved in some parasite lifecycles. This increases the transmission rate as it allows the parasite to spread, even when the infected host is incapacitated. For example, the mosquito can spread the *Plasmodium* parasite from people who are immobilised due to a malarial fever.

Some parasites have **waterborne dispersal stages** which take advantage of the liquid medium to disperse and transmit to new hosts. For example, cholera victims are quickly immobilised by the disease, but their waste transmits the bacterium back into the water supply, where it can be taken in by new hosts.

Host behaviour is often exploited and modified by parasites

Some parasites **exploit the natural behaviours** of the hosts to maximise transmission. For example, *Schistosoma* exploits the behaviour of mammals which wade into lakes. The parasite is released from an aquatic snail (intermediate host), so it has a waterborne dispersal stage which can burrow into the skin of the legs of new hosts in the water.

The **host's behaviour can be modified** by infection so that the parasite is passed on more easily. In this case, the host behaviour becomes part of the **extended phenotype** of the parasite and there are five key categories of behaviour modification.

Category of behaviour modified	Host and parasite	Extended phenotype
Foraging	Mosquito and *Plasmodium*	Mosquito with mature parasites is more likely to feed on blood from more than one person
Movement	Frogs and flatworm	Frog develops additional back legs, so moves slower and is more easily caught by the next host (predatory bird)
Sexual behaviour	Mayfly and nematode	Parasite has to return to water to find its next host (fish) so mayfly females go to lay eggs even if no eggs present; males behave like females and attempt to lay eggs
Habitat choice	Ant and flatworm	Ant climbs to top of blade of grass at night, instead of going to nest, so is eaten by its next host (deer or sheep)
Anti-predator behaviour	Rats and *Toxoplasma*	Rat seeks out the smell of cat urine, so is eaten by cat and parasite is ingested by new host

FACTORS THAT INCREASE VIRULENCE

A parasite with a high transmission rate will experience selection pressure for increased virulence, increasing **parasite growth** and **reproduction** in the host. There are three major ways that endoparasites achieve this. They:

1. suppress the **host immune system** so that parasites survive and reproduce in the host without being attacked by the host's defences

contd

2. modify the **size of the host** so that it grows much larger and can support the asexual reproduction of more parasites, e.g. infected mud snails in Asia grow about 25% larger

3. reduce the host's **reproductive rate** so more of the host's energy can be directed to parasite reproduction, e.g. *Sacculina* is a parasitic barnacle that destroys the gonads of its crab host.

DON'T FORGET

The parasite reaches sexual maturity in (or on) the definitive host. The intermediate host is needed for the parasite to complete its lifecycle.

LIFECYCLES AND HOSTS

Some parasites have only one host species

Some parasites that use direct contact as their transmission mechanism can complete their lifecycle within one host species. Many of these are ectoparasites or endoparasites of the main body cavities (such as the gut or lungs).

- Ectoparasitic arthropods (e.g. human head lice) go from egg through to full reproductive maturity on a single host. This is why the removal of adult head lice and eggs demands repeated combing over a number of weeks. Transmission is achieved by adults moving to new hosts in close proximity.

- One species of human tapeworm completes its lifecycle from start to finish in the large intestine of their human hosts. Transmission is achieved using cysts in faeces; these cysts are taken up by the next host in contaminated food or water.

Many parasites need more than one host species

Some parasites have to spend part of their lifecycle in an intermediate host species to complete their lifecycle, so that they are better able to be transmitted to a new definitive host.

Some ectoparasite and some endoparasite species have increased their transmission efficiency by having a lifecycle stage in an intermediate host. Transmission is achieved when the definitive host **consumes the intermediate host**. For example, the eggs of the pork tapeworm are passed out from a person in the faeces and the eggs are eaten by pigs (the intermediate host). The eggs hatch and develop as cysts in the muscle tissue, before being consumed by a human. Beef tapeworm are transmitted in the same way while fish tapeworm need an additional intermediate host.

Endoparasites of the body tissues are often transmitted by **vectors** which play an active part in the transmission, so helping to increase the transmission efficiency. In the case of *Plasmodium*, the mosquito is both definitive host and vector. *Schistosoma* are also endoparasites of body tissues but the snail is not a vector in the lifecycle as it has no active role in the transmission; these parasites use waterborne stages to increase their transmission efficiency.

DON'T FORGET

Vectors play an active role in the transmission of the parasite.

Lifecycles of four species of human tapeworm. One species relies on direct re-infection, while three species require intermediate hosts. None of the lifecycles have vectors.

DON'T FORGET

The only parasitic lifecycles that you need to know are those of *Plasmodium* and *Schistosoma*.

 THINGS TO DO AND THINK ABOUT

Public-health measures often try to reduce the transmission of parasites. If these measures are successful, what long-term effect will this have on the virulence of the parasite? This effect was observed in cholera outbreaks in South America: when cholera invaded countries with poor water sanitation, the strains evolved to be more virulent, while strains that invaded areas with better sanitation evolved to be less harmful.

ONLINE TEST

Test yourself on transmission and virulence at www.brightredbooks.net

MAMMALIAN IMMUNE RESPONSE

Mammals have evolved a layered defence against parasites. The first and second line of defences are **non-specific** and work against of a wide range of parasites. The third line is a cellular response that is **specific**, because it attacks the antigens of the parasite. However, the battle may not be won by the host as parasites have evolved their own strategies to evade host defences.

NON-SPECIFIC DEFENCES

First-line defences

These are **physical barriers** and **chemical secretions** that work together to prevent many parasites from entering the body fluids. **Physical barriers:** Epithelial tissue blocks the entry of parasites; it is also dry, so many microbial parasites die on the surface. Nasal hairs trap many microbial parasites and prevent them from contacting the delicate tissues in the lungs.

Chemical secretions: Mucus in the lungs traps microbial parasites. The mucus is continuously moved away from delicate alveolar tissue by the action of cilia. Hydrolytic enzymes in mucus, saliva and tears destroy bacterial cell walls. The cellular proteins of pathogens are denatured by the low pH environments of the secretions of the stomach, vagina and sweat glands.

Second-line defences

Second-line defences (inflammatory response, phagocytes and natural killer cells) happen as a response after a parasite has entered the body fluids. They are produced quite rapidly without the need to determine the invader's identity. These non-specific responses are the **inflammatory response**, **phagocytes** and **natural killer cells** (see table below).

Some of the phagocytes remain active. After they have engulfed and digested the foreign object, they present **fragments of the foreign antigens** on their surface. This will be important as part of the immune surveillance in the next stage of defence.

Inflammatory response	Phagocytes	Natural killer cells
Some injured or infected cells can release signalling molecules including **histamine**.	These are white blood cells which are able to migrate out from the blood into the tissue fluid which surrounds cells. The phagocytes can engulf bacteria, viruses and dust particles into a vacuole.	These are also a type of white blood cell which can migrate into the tissue fluid. They detect the **abnormal cell-surface proteins** found on virus-infected cells and on cancerous cells.
This causes the local blood vessels to dilate, so enhancing the blood flow to the area, making it become red and warm.	The phagocytes check the surfaces of cells and particles for 'self' antigens. If these are not found, then the phagocyte **engulfs and digests** the foreign object using powerful enzymes contained in lysosomes. This process is phagocytosis.	The natural killer cells do not engulf the stricken cell but, instead, attach to it and release chemicals into it. These chemicals induce the cell to kill itself, a process called **apoptosis**.
The permeability of the blood vessels also increases, so fluid moves into the tissue, which swells up; this puts pressure on nerve endings leading to pain in the area.		
This swelling also brings antimicrobial proteins and stimulates **phagocytes** to migrate to the area.	Many phagocytes die at the site of their action and form the pus that is found at an infected wound.	Phagocytes engulf and digest the resulting cell debris.

SPECIFIC CELLULAR DEFENCES

The third line of defences is triggered by the antigens on the surface of the parasite. The responses at this stage are specific to these antigens and involve lymphocytes. A range of white blood cells constantly circulates, monitoring the tissues. If tissues become damaged or invaded, cells release cytokines that increase blood flow resulting in non-specific and specific white blood cells accumulating at the site of infection or tissue damage.

Lymphocytes and immune surveillance

Lymphocytes are white blood cells which are found mainly in the lymph glands. Lymphocytes each present only one type of **antigen-receptor protein** on their surface and these can bind to just one specific antigen. Although each of us can produce between 1 million and 10 million different antigen receptors, each lymphocyte can make only one type of receptor. This is because each lymphocyte is part of a **clone**, a group of about 1000 identical cells made from a common ancestral cell, which was committed to produce a single type of antigen receptor.

DON'T FORGET

Specific defences are produced in response to the presence of a specific antigen.

Tissue fluid is drained from the around the body's cells by the lymphatic system. The lymph fluid passes through the lymph glands, where the lymphocytes carry out **immune surveillance**, checking for their specific antigens using the receptor proteins on their surface. During this surveillance, phagocytes in the lymph fluid are also checked for their presented antigen fragments.

VIDEO LINK

An animated summary of the immune system can be found at www.brightredbooks.net

Clonal selection and the action of lymphocytes

The specific lymphocyte clones undergo **clonal selection** when their antigen-receptor proteins bind to their specific antigen. This activates the lymphocytes, making them ready to divide rapidly to produce many more clones, each with the same specific antigen receptor.

Some of these **lymphocytes** produce **antibodies**. Antibodies possess regions where the amino acid sequence varies greatly between different antibodies. The variable region gives the antibody its specificity for binding antigen. These antibodies bind to the antigens on the parasite. The antigen–antibody complex formed can inactivate the parasite, making it easier for the phagocytes to find and engulf, or it can cause the parasite cell to undergo lysis.

Other **lymphocytes** destroy infected cells by inducing **apoptosis**. (Although this is a similar function to that of the natural killer cells, these lymphocytes are much more effective but can only attack a cell if it has the specific antigen.)

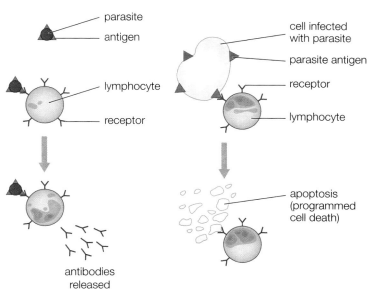

Some lymphocytes produce antibodies

Immunological memory

Once the parasite infection has been defeated, some members of the lymphocyte clones are kept as an **immunological memory**. The **long-term survival** of a larger population of these memory lymphocyte cells means that they produce a quicker and larger response if the specific antigen is detected again. This is the basis of immunisations, whereby an antigen is presented to the immune system using a harmless version of the parasite.

Initial antigen exposure produces **memory lymphocyte** cells specific for that antigen that can produce a secondary response when the same antigen enters the body in the future. When this occurs, antibody production is enhanced in terms of speed of production, concentration in blood and duration.

ONLINE TEST

Test yourself on the mammalian immune response to parasites at www.brightredbooks.net

IMMUNE EVASION

The ongoing Red Queen's race between the parasite and host means that some endoparasites have evolved ways to evade the immune system.

1. Mimic host antigens – hide from the immune system	2. Antigenic variation – be a moving target for the immune system	3. Integrate genome into host genome
Schistosoma produces surface antigens that mimic those of the human host. This helps it to evade detection by the immune system and so there is a reduced antibody response by the host and reduced chance of parasite destruction.	*Plasmodium* have hundreds of copies of surface-antigen genes and each new generation expresses a new, randomly selected set of these antigen genes. This allows the parasite to evolve quicker than the host immune system can respond, so the parasite is always one step ahead. This may also allow re-infection of the same host with the new variant.	Some viruses escape immune surveillance by integrating their genome into host genomes, existing in an inactive state known as latency. The virus becomes active again when favourable conditions arise.

THINGS TO DO AND THINK ABOUT

Nettle stings produce a very quick inflammatory response, because the sting contains histamine which automatically causes the body's inflammation response. The sting also injects acetyl choline and serotonin, which are neurotransmitters that cause the intense pain of a nettle sting.

TREATMENT AND CONTROL OF PARASITES

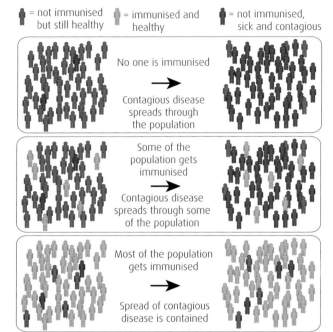

= not immunised but still healthy

= immunised and healthy

= not immunised, sick and contagious

No one is immunised

Contagious disease spreads through the population

Some of the population gets immunised

Contagious disease spreads through some of the population

Most of the population gets immunised

Spread of contagious disease is contained

Herd immunity.

EPIDEMIOLOGY

Epidemiology is the study of the **outbreak and spread of infectious disease**. The information gained from epidemiological surveys can be used to plan and evaluate strategies to prevent the spread of the parasite in future.

One way to prevent the spread of disease is to use vaccinations to increase the number of resistant hosts in the population; to create **herd immunity**. This occurs when any new infection in a population can be contained because susceptible hosts are too dispersed for the parasite to continue to spread. The **herd-immunity threshold** is the density of resistant hosts required in a population to prevent an epidemic.

Many vaccination programs aim to reach the herd-immunity threshold as this protects any individuals who cannot have the vaccination for health reasons. This is particularly important in less economically developed countries, where poorer nutrition weakens the health of individuals so they are more susceptible to diseases and their complications.

PROBLEMS IN TREATING PARASITIC DISEASES

Vaccination

Vaccination exposes the immune system to a non-infectious source of parasite antigens. This elicits an immune response and develops immunological memory to these antigens and so protects against infection by the real parasite. This is a relatively straightforward concept, but developing a new vaccine is not so easy in practice.

Some parasites (e.g. *Schistosoma*) are **difficult to culture** in the laboratory because they need a very narrow range of conditions, as well as specific host signals for their development. This makies it difficult to develop vaccines.

The parasite may use **rapid antigen change** as a means of evading the immune system (e.g. *Plasmodium*) and this makes **vaccine design very complex;** a vaccine would have to reflect this antigenic variation.

Drugs

The similarities between **host and parasite metabolism** make it difficult to find drug compounds that **only target the parasite**.

Drugs that work to kill the parasite in the host could have detrimental effects on the host. This was a major problem with early antiparasitic drugs, which were difficult to administer in effective doses that were still safe to the patient. These problems meant that only 0·1% of all new drugs from 1975 to 1999 were antiparasitics.

Investment by charities and use of molecular-biology techniques has increased the number of antiparasitic drugs being found, but they are still a tiny minority of medicines under development. Most parasitic diseases are prevalent only in the poorer parts of the world, so there has been little possibility of pharmaceutical companies recouping the huge investment costs of developing a new drug.

VIDEO LINK

Check out the clip about herd immunity at www.brightredbooks.net

ONLINE

Read about the near success of polio vaccination programmes and worries about a lack of herd immunity in Europe at www.brightredbooks.net

DON'T FORGET

You need to know the definition of herd-immunity threshold.

DON'T FORGET

You need to know the two problems associated with developing antiparasitic drugs.

contd

A further problem is that drugs provide a selection pressure, leading to the evolution of resistant strains of parasites. New drugs are used in carefully planned combinations so that, even if the parasite could resist one drug, it will be killed by the others.

ONLINE

Learn more about the unsettling possible side effects of antimalarial drugs at www.brightredbooks.net

CONTROLLING PARASITES

Successful parasites are always running in the Red Queen's biological race so, while our medical efforts against them may give us the upper hand in the short term, it is likely that many parasites will continue to evolve countermeasures. In many situations, it may be that the only effective control strategy is to attack the parasite indirectly, by working on ways to reduce the spread of parasites.

Targetting transmission

Many parasites use waterborne stages or vectors to increase their transmission rate, so these are potential targets. If effective, blocking these may have the added benefit that they act against other parasites that use the same transmission routes.

1. **Civil-engineering projects** (such as installing toilet facilities, sewerage systems and water taps from boreholes) all work to **improve sanitation**. These prevent the mixing of drinking water with water that is contaminated by human waste, blocking the transmission route for many different parasites, such as cholera bacteria and *Schistosoma*.

ONLINE

Who has invested a billion dollars of their own money to help combat parasitic diseases? Find out at www.brightredbooks.net

2. Using a **coordinated vector-control strategy** can be highly effective. Measures to reduce the spread of malaria include spraying houses with insecticide to kill mosquitos and using bed nets to prevent access of mosquitos to people at night. These have also reduced the spread of other mosquito-borne diseases like Dengue fever, yellow fever and elephantiasis.

Reducing the transmission rate may be very difficult in situations where parasites have conditions that help them to **spread rapidly**. Challenges arise in parasite control as a result of **overcrowding** (e.g. in refugee camps that result from war or natural disaster or in rapidly growing cities in LEDCs) and **tropical climates** where the parasites can spread most rapidly in warm environmental conditions.

MALARIA KILLS A CHILD EVERY 60 SECONDS

Text £3. Send a net. Save a life.

Benefits of improving parasite control

Many charities run campaigns that rightly focus on the terrible effects of parasitic infections on individuals. These charities invest in better parasite-control measures and so greatly **reduce child mortality**, but there are wider benefits to the population. The general health of children is greatly improved, since their bodily resources are not being redirected to support the parasite. The children, therefore, have **more resources for growth and development** and, since more children are healthy, this leads to **population-wide improvements** in **child development and intelligence**.

Charity campaigns aim at our individual sensibilities, but the effect of the charities' actions are much deeper and broader.

THINGS TO DO AND THINK ABOUT

The parasite-control double whammy
Parasite virulence is high in a population with poor health. Improving the health of the population through better nutrition, hygiene and sanitation is an effective way to reduce virulence. Better hygiene and sanitation also reduce the rate of transmission – and lower transmission rates force the parasite to evolve lower virulence.

ONLINE TEST

Head to www.brightredbooks.net to test yourself on the treatment and control of parasites.

SCIENTIFIC METHOD AND ETHICS

THE SCIENTIFIC CYCLE

Scientific knowledge is constantly evolving and changing as new data is generated, leading to refinement of our ideas. Scientific knowledge can be thought of as the current best explanation, which may then be updated after evaluation of further experimental evidence. The scientific cycle is a series of steps that biologists use to investigate phenomena in a **testable**, **measurable** and **reproducible** way, with the ultimate aim of explaining and predicting future observations by refining a **hypothesis**.

Construction of a hypothesis

A hypothesis is a potential explanation for an observed event, or a predicted outcome for a proposed experimental procedure. It must be possible to test a hypothesis using the steps in the scientific cycle and it should allow prediction of future events. The **null hypothesis** will be no statistically significant effect as a result of the experimental treatment. If there is evidence for an effect, unlikely due to chance, then the null hypothesis is rejected.

Stages in the scientific cycle.

Experimental design

Design of experiments must provide data to confirm or refute the hypothesis. Care should be taken to ensure experiments are **reproducible**, **reliable**, include both **negative** and **positive control groups** where appropriate, and make sure all important **confounding variables** are kept constant or monitored.

Gathering and recording of data

Raw data should be recorded to an appropriate degree of accuracy, which is determined by the scale of measurements being made, limitations of equipment and a balance between cost, time and the number of measurements required for statistical analysis.

Analysis of data

Once gathered, data should be analysed to determine whether conclusions can be formulated. Analysis of experimental data should include consideration of the accuracy and precision of measurements, of the number of replicates and may also include an appropriate statistical test.

Determination of conclusions

After data analysis, it should be decided whether the data supports the hypothesis or if a new hypothesis should be proposed to explain the results. It is important to recognise that failure to find an effect (a negative result) is a **valid finding** if the experiment was well designed. Conflicting data or conclusions can be resolved through careful evaluation or can lead to further experimentation. Scientific ideas only become accepted once they have been checked independently. Effects must be reproducible; one-off results are treated with caution.

SCIENTIFIC ETHICS

Ethics can be thought of as the rules for distinguishing between right and wrong. All science should be carried out with a strong ethical basis, given the power of science to impact on society and the environment.

contd

Personal ethics of the scientist

Scientists must behave with integrity and honesty. As such, results should be presented in an **unbiased** way by including all data.

Scientists should always acknowledge the contributions of others to their work. Where previous studies are quoted or summarised, the original author must be cited and referenced. A **citation** is an acknowledgement that appears in the text where the work of another scientist is being described or quoted. A list of **references** for all citations should be included in any scientific writing and must contain enough information to allow readers to find the original publication. Appropriate use of citations and references is essential for avoiding **plagiarism**. Judgement and interpretations of evidence may be disputed, and replication of experiments by others reduces the opportunities for dishonesty or deliberate misuse of science.

Ethics of animal studies

Many biological studies require the use of animal experimentation, due to the complex and interdependent nature of different cells and systems which cannot always be modelled outside the body. The use of animals for research is controversial and, as such, scientists should be governed by the principles of **Replacement**, **Reduction** and **Refinement**:

Scientific ethics.

Replacement – avoid using animals when an alternative cellular or model system exists.

Reduction – reduce the number of animals in a study (without compromising the validity or reliability).

Refinement – techniques should be adjusted to minimise harm to the animals.

Ethics of human studies

Any experimentation on humans is governed by four key principles:

1. Participants should be given details of the study to enable them to agree to take part, known as giving their **informed consent**.

2. Participants have the **right to withdraw data** and their participation at any point during the study.

3. Any data gathered should be anonymous and kept **confidential**.

4. Lastly, studies should aim to ensure that participants come to **no harm** from the study.

Ethics of funding and approving studies

Scientists are not free to investigate any scientific question that interests them. They must justify their research in terms of benefits of its outcome, and assess any risks to species, investigators and the environment. The overall direction of science is controlled by legislation, regulation, policy and funding priorities. Legislation limits the potential for misuse of studies and data. There are several regulatory bodies that have oversight of specific areas of scientific research in the UK, e.g. human stem cell research is governed by the Human Fertilisation and Embryology Authority and studies involving patients are approved by the Health Research Authority.

 ONLINE

Find out more about citing and referencing at www.brightredbooks.net

 DON'T FORGET

Any definitive statement should be cited and referenced. If you ever find this information is missing, you should question the reliability of the statement.

 ONLINE

Find out more about the ethics of human experimentation by reading the Nuremberg Code (1947) at www.brightredbooks.net

THINGS TO DO AND THINK ABOUT

1. For the following aims, write a possible hypothesis and the relevant null hypothesis.
   a) To investigate the effect of light intensity on the rate of photosynthesis in *Elodea*.
   b) To investigate the effect of listening to different types of music on reaction times of students.
   c) To determine the effect of increasing concentrations of caffeine on heart rate in humans.
2. Use the ethics diagram to create a mind map summarising the various ethical considerations involved in carrying out scientific research.

SCIENTIFIC LITERATURE AND COMMUNICATION

Science involves the sharing of findings so that data and ideas can be evaluated by others. Scientists do not accept new ideas without being able to evaluate methods, data and its analysis, and conclusions. One of the key concepts of modern science is that sufficient information should be communicated to allow others to repeat an experiment to **verify results** and **conclusions**.

TYPES OF SCIENTIFIC PUBLICATION

There are two types of formal scientific publication: primary papers and review articles.

Primary papers communicate new research findings and should include:

- an explanatory **title**

- a **summary** containing aims and findings (also known as an **abstract**). The **aim** should clearly state the independent variable (the variable being controlled and deliberately changed), the dependent variable (the variable that the hypothesis states will be affected by altering the independent variable) and the organism, system or molecule being studied

- an **introduction** which explains the purpose and context of the study. Introductions should make use of a variety of sources to support the current study, and must be properly cited and referenced. The introduction should also contain the author's hypothesis

- a **method** section that contains **sufficient information to allow other scientists to repeat the experiments**. The method should clearly define the independent and dependent variables in the study

- a **results** section that includes all relevant **raw data**, **processed data** in the form of summary graphs or tables, and a clear explanation of how the authors have **analysed** the data

- **conclusions** that are supported by the data and refer to the aim and hypothesis. A discussion of the validity and reliability of experimental design should also take place here

- **references** for all cited work

Review articles are used to summarise the current knowledge in a particular field and to discuss recent or novel findings. Review articles are usually written by experts in that area of study and provide an 'up-to-the-minute' account of an area of science.

DON'T FORGET

Common methods of sharing original scientific findings include seminars, talks and posters at conferences, as well as publishing in academic journals.

DON'T FORGET

If a primary scientific publication is lacking any of the described sections, the overall findings of the paper should be treated with caution.

PEER REVIEW AND CRITICAL EVALUATION

A key step in scientific publishing is peer review. This is when scientific papers are read and analysed by specialists with expertise in the relevant field of study. The reviewers assess the scientific quality of the submitted manuscript and make recommendations regarding its suitability for publication. Often, the paper will not be published without the author first responding to the reviewer's comments. Examples of peer reviewers' requests include:

- alterations to experimental design, such as better control of confounding variables
- increased numbers of replicates
- additional experiments
- different or more suitable data analysis
- inclusion of missing key background information.

Only after successful peer review will papers be accepted and published in scientific journals. However, even if a report has been accepted by reviewers, individual readers should always be **critical** in reading and **evaluating** scientific research.

DON'T FORGET

Scientists should be critical when evaluating any piece of research. If you cannot access or find references, methods or data, you cannot be sure that the conclusions are valid.

SCIENCE REPORTING IN THE MEDIA

Most people do not gain scientific knowledge by accessing formal scientific publications, but instead gain information from the wider media. The wider media is not subject to peer review, so it is important to critically evaluate this type of scientific coverage. In addition, science that is reported in the wider media usually does not include methods and data; sometimes it is not even clear where the report is published or who the authors are. This can lead to misinterpretation of the significance of results and to overhyping of new scientific discoveries. To address the issue of misrepresentation of science there are great efforts to increase the public understanding of science.

NEW STERILISATION RULES WOULD COST MILLIONS

Surgery spread AIDS

Could your fridge KILL YOU?

IS SWINE FLU ALREADY HERE?

THINGS TO DO AND THINK ABOUT

1 Access some primary scientific papers using www.ncbi.nlm.nih.gov/pubmed **or** journals.plos.org/plosone/ and attempt to identify the following:
   a) the authors
   b) the authors' institute or university
   c) the time taken to peer review (difference between date submitted and date accepted)
   d) the independent and dependent variables
   e) the aim
   f) the hypothesis
   g) evidence of citations and references in background information.

2 Read a recent newspaper article describing a scientific story. Can you identify from the article the authors of the study, where it was published, the methods used and the data that conclusions are based on?

ONLINE

Find out about the roles played by scientists, the media and society in the MMR vaccine scare at www.brightredbooks.net

SCIENTIFIC EXPERIMENTATION 1

PILOT STUDY

A **pilot study** is integral to the development of a scientific investigation. The purpose of the pilot study is to develop and improve experimental protocols, ensuring that the experimental design is suitable for investigating the aim and hypothesis. The use of pilot studies is necessary to avoid wasting significant time and money on full-scale investigations using flawed experimental methods. A pilot study should be used to provide information and data on a number of parts of experimental design, as summarised on the right.

EXPERIMENTAL VARIABLES

In an experiment, the experimental treatment group is compared to a control group. However, in any biological experiment, there is usually a large number of factors that can change, known as variables. Experimental variables can be split into three types, **independent**, **dependent** and **confounding** (see next page).

Independent variable

The **independent variable** is the variable that is deliberately changed by the investigator to determine if it has an effect on the outcome of the experiment. Experiments can be **simple**, changing only one independent variable, or **multifactorial**, changing more than one independent variable. In **observational studies**, a variable that already exists within the study population is selected and is considered to be the independent variable (see page 96).

Dependent variable

A **dependent variable** is a variable that is measured to determine if changing the independent variable has an effect.

Assess validity of experimental design	Validity is the term used to cover the overall experimental concept; to be valid, variables must be controlled so that any measured effect is likely to be due to the independent variable. The pilot study is an opportunity to measure how well confounding variables are kept constant and to consider if the experimental design has failed to control any important confounding variables. Validity includes considering if the experiment has sufficient control groups and appropriate randomisation of experimental subjects.
Plan procedures and check techniques	The pilot study allows the investigator to decide if the experimental approach, procedures and techniques are suitable for investigating the aim. The experimental protocol should be evaluated to determine whether measurements are made with an acceptable degree of **accuracy** and **precision**. The pilot study is also an opportunity for the investigator to practise difficult or unfamiliar techniques.
Determine a suitable range of values for the independent variable	It is common to use a linear or log **dilution series** in pilot studies to find out an appropriate range of values for the independent variable. Data from the pilot study allows selection of a range of values for the independent variable that provide an effect on the dependent variable, while avoiding an overly large number of experimental groups.
Identify suitable numbers of repeat measurements for each independent data point	Biological data, by its nature, is variable. In order to be able to come to a **reliable** conclusion, not only is a sufficient sample required, but every data point needs to have been the result of repeated measures. The pilot study will provide data allowing a decision to be made on the number of replicates required to ensure data is representative.

Importance of a pilot study.

Type of experimental design	Examples	Advantages	Disadvantages
Simple	Commonly laboratory-based studies	• Simpler experimental design • Variables are tightly controlled • Results easy to analyse and interpret	• Difficult to extrapolate results to whole organisms or environments • Not suitable for testing complex hypotheses
Multifactorial	Field studies, whole-organism (*in vivo*) studies	• Allows examination of complex interactions • Allows generalisations to be made • Results applicable to study environment or organism	• More complex and time consuming • Difficult to control all variables • Analysis of data is complex

Comparison of simple and multifactorial studies.

Types of variables and data

Variables can be classed as either **discrete** or **continuous** data.

- **Discrete variables** have finite values that allow placement into separate groups, for example sex, number of pets in a household, or number of students in a class.

contd

- **Continuous variables** change gradually from one extreme to another, potentially having an infinite number of possible values. Examples of continuous variables include height, age, and concentration.

Key concept	Explanation
Validity	Variables must be controlled so that any measured effect is likely to be due to the independent variable.
Reliability	Consistent values in repeats and independent replicates.
Accuracy	Data, or means of data sets, are close to the true value.
Precision	Measured values are close to each other.

OBSERVATIONAL STUDIES

In some contexts, such as epidemiology or psychology studies, it can be difficult for investigators to control the independent variable directly, due to ethical concerns or the logistics involved in creating randomised experimental groups. For example, if a scientist wanted to study the effects of smoking on heart disease, it would be unethical, extremely expensive and time consuming to recruit two groups of people and have one group start smoking for a number of years to compare the effects to a control group of non-smokers. Instead, investigators may carry out **observational studies**, using groups that already exist at the expense of being unable to control the independent variable (e.g. smokers and non-smokers). In observational studies there is no truly independent variable.

Observational studies using existing groups are good at detecting **correlations** between two variables. **Correlations** may be **positive** – as one variable increases the other variable increases too – or **negative**, whereby one variable increases as the other variable decreases. The dispersion of the points about the line of best fit gives an indication of the variability of the data and the strength of the correlation, if many points are far from the line then the correlation is weak. Although observational studies can show correlations between two variables, care should be taken in assigning **causation** as observational studies do not directly test a hypothesis.

Positive Correlation

Negative Correlation

No Correlation

Example of positive and negative correlation. Experimental studies, where the independent variable is directly manipulated by the experimentor, are required in order to identify causation.

 THINGS TO DO AND THINK ABOUT

1   For each of the following experiments list the confounding variables that should be controlled and the type of data that will be obtained.
   a) An investigation into the effect of temperature on the rate of respiration in yeast.
   b) To determine the effect of age on blood pressure in humans.
   c) An investigation of the antimicrobial properties of garlic paste on growth rates of *E. coli*.
   d) The effect of nitrogen concentration on root length of cress plants.

DON'T FORGET

The purpose of a pilot study is to verify experimental protocols and methods, before starting a large-scale investigation. It is normal and expected to use data from a pilot study to alter and improve experimental design.

VIDEO LINK

Watch the clip at www.brightredbooks.net to find out more about discrete and continuous variables.

DON'T FORGET

The type of variable being measured determines the appropriate graphical display or statistical test that should be used.

DON'T FORGET

Correlation does not mean that changing one variable *results* in the other variable changing (causation). Only when all confounding variables are controlled, can correlation be proved to demonstrate causation.

SCIENTIFIC EXPERIMENTATION 2

CONFOUNDING VARIABLES

A **confounding variable** is a variable, other than the independent variable, that may affect the dependent variable. As biological systems are complex, most biological experiments contain many confounding variables. A valid experimental design should seek to keep all confounding variables constant if possible, or monitor them so that their effect on the results can be accounted for in the analysis.

If confounding variables cannot be controlled effectively, then a **randomised block design** may be used to minimise the effect of uncontrolled confounding variables.

Randomised block design

In an experiment to test the effect of sex on heart rate in humans, there are many confounding variables that may affect the results, for example age, height, weight, fitness. It would be extremely difficult to control these variables as the researcher would need to find sufficient numbers of subjects all of the same age, height, weight and fitness levels. Therefore, the subjects are grouped (or blocked) randomly, so that the male and female groups contain a similar range of ages, heights, weights and fitness levels. Randomised block design is a form of stratified sampling (see page 103).

Randomised blocks of treatment and control groups can be disturbed in such a way that the influence of any confounding variables is likely to be the same across the treatment and control groups.

ONLINE

Read more about control groups at www.brightredbooks.net

DON'T FORGET

If either the negative or positive control groups give unexpected results, the experiment is not valid and any results obtained cannot be interpreted.

CONTROL GROUPS

In any scientific experiment, control groups should be included to enable comparison of the results of experimental treatment group with the results of controls. It is only by comparing the treatment group's results with control group results that the experimental design can be shown to be valid. There are two types of experimental control group, **negative controls** and **positive controls**.

Negative control group	The negative control group provides data for what happens in the absence of a treatment. It is carried out to check false positive results are not occurring. The negative control should show that the dependent variable remains stable, within an expected range, when the independent variable is absent or constant. If the negative control gives unexpected results, it is likely that a confounding variable is not adequately controlled.
Positive control group	The positive control group provides data to prove that the experimental design can detect a positive result when one occurs. It is carried out to check whether false negative results are occurring. If the positive control shows no effect on the dependent variable, the experimental design is not valid and requires refinement.

Example: Testing the effectiveness of a new disinfectant

In an experiment to test the ability of a new disinfectant to control growth of bacteria, the investigators grow bacteria on an agar plate that is supplemented with the disinfectant. After 24 hours' incubation the number of bacterial colonies is counted. In this experiment, the negative control would be an agar plate inoculated with bacteria but containing no disinfectant. The positive control is an inoculated agar plate containing a different disinfectant that is known to kill bacteria. Expected results are shown below.

Negative control
agar + bacteria + no disinfectant
Shows normal bacterial growth.

Treatment group
agar + bacteria + new disinfectant
Shows some bacterial growth depending on effectiveness of new disinfectant and concentration tested.

Positive control
agar + bacteria + other disinfectant
Shows little or no bacterial growth

Example of negative and positive control group expected results.

contd

Example: Use of placebos and the placebo effect

Another type of control is a placebo, and this is used as a control for the effect of a patient's expectations.

A placebo can be included as a treatment without the presence of the independent variable being investigated. The patient would be unaware (blinded) as to whether they were receiving treatment or placebo. The placebo effect is a measurable change in the dependent variable as a result of a patient's expectations, rather than changes in the independent variable.

Advantages and disadvantages of *in vivo* and *in vitro* studies

In biological studies, experiments generally fall into two types: *in vivo* and *in vitro*. *In vivo* is Latin for 'within the living', and is the term used to describe studies involving whole living organisms. *In vitro* is Latin for 'in glass', and is the term used to describe laboratory studies using isolated components of organisms, e.g. enzymes or proteins, or cells growing in culture medium. *In vitro* refers to the technique of performing a given procedure in a controlled environment outside of a living organism.

Type of study	Advantages	Disadvantages
In vivo	• Provide data for effects in whole organisms • Allows study of complex interactions	• Expensive and time consuming • Ethical and legislative concerns • Difficult to control confounding variables • Results may be difficult to interpret • Difficult to prove causation
In vitro	• Simpler and less expensive • Easier to control confounding variables • Interpretation of results is simpler • Can demonstrate correlation and causation	• Difficult to extend results to whole organism or different species • Difficult to model complex interactions

ONLINE

Read more about examples of correlations that do not show causation at www.brightredbooks.net

EVALUATING EXPERIMENTAL DESIGN

Evaluating experimental design is a complex activity and requires consideration of a number of factors. As a reader you should assess the experimental design for **validity** and **reliability**. This should include consideration of:

- the suitability of the experimental approach for testing the given aim and hypothesis. If the design is unsuitable, the experiment is invalid

- control groups. **Treatment effects must be compared to effects in control groups.** If either negative or positive controls are missing or give unexpected results, the results must be interpreted with extreme caution and may be dismissed

- adequate **control of confounding variables**. Where confounding variables cannot be controlled, they must be monitored and their contribution to changes in the dependent variable considered

- **selection bias**. This results in non-random and unrepresentative groups and should be avoided. Selection bias happens when the individuals who are selected for a study are not representative of the population as a whole

- **sample size**. This is the number of tests or individuals in treatment and control groups. Sample size should be large enough to allow results to be tested statistically and should aim to be as near to a representative sample as the method allows.

DON'T FORGET

When evaluating experimental design, it is necessary to identify the independent, dependent and all important confounding variables. If the method does not explain how all these variables were measured or controlled, it is likely that the experimental design is not valid.

THINGS TO DO AND THINK ABOUT

1. Design suitable negative and positive controls for the laboratory techniques from Unit 1 below:
   a) Colorimetry to determine the concentration of an unknown
   b) Thin-layer chromatography to separate photosynthetic pigments
   c) Separation of proteins by gel electrophoresis
   d) ELISA
   e) Viable cell counting using a vital stain.

2. Write a paragraph to explain why both *in vivo* and *in vitro* studies are used in biology.

SAMPLING AND RELIABILITY

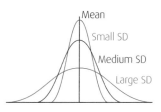

Mean
Small SD
Medium SD
Large SD

Comparison of low-variation and high-variation population distributions. This figure compares normally distributed data sets with low (blue), medium (black) and high (red) variation. The variation is measured by calculating the standard deviation. A representative sample of the red population would require more individual samples than a representative sample of the blue population.

SAMPLING

In an ideal world, biological studies would gather data from all individuals within a population. However, this is often impractical due to time and cost considerations. Biologists, therefore, conduct experiments on a **representative sample** of a population and seek to extrapolate their results to the population as a whole.

In order for a sample to be representative, it must take into account the extent of natural variation in the population and how the population as a whole is distributed. The greater the variation in the population, the larger the sample size required. Overall, a representative sample should have the **same mean** and **same degree of variation about the mean** as the population as a whole.

TYPES OF SAMPLING

There are three main types of sampling strategy: random, systematic and stratified:

- **Random sampling** allows each member of the population to have an equal chance of being selected. It is non-subjective and shows little or no bias in selecting samples. Random sampling should use random number tables or random number generators to select samples. Random sampling is used for sampling very large areas or populations with relatively uniform distributions.

- **Systematic sampling** selects members of a population at regular intervals. For example, in a transect study of plants, a quadrat would be taken at every metre along the transect; when sampling humans, every fifth person in a population could be sampled.

- **Stratified sampling** divides the population into categories that are then sampled proportionally. Stratified sampling is used when the population being sampled is not uniform. The population is made up of subsets of known sizes and the number of samples taken from each subset is proportional to and representative of the whole population. An example of stratified sampling would be measuring the abundance of plants in an area of grassland. Certain plants may grow in patches that might be missed by random sampling, whereas stratified sampling would ensure these areas are sampled proportionally.

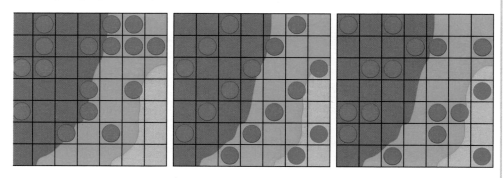

Random, systematic and stratified sampling.

Ensuring reliability

The natural variability of biological material and populations often leads to variation in experimental results, especially when studying whole organisms or populations but even with purified molecules.

Although such variation is to be expected, investigators should also consider the contribution of experimental design and measurement methods in producing

 contd

variable results. In order to have confidence in results, care should be taken to ensure that repeated measurements are taken and that any measurement methods are suitably **precise, accurate, and reliable**.

PRECISION AND ACCURACY OF REPEATED MEASUREMENTS

When designing an experiment, consideration should be given to the degree of precision and accuracy required to detect differences in key variables. The reliability of measuring instruments or procedures can be determined by repeated measurements of an individual datum point. The variation observed indicates the precision of the measurement, instrument or procedure, but not necessarily its accuracy.

- **Precision** is a measurement of the closeness of two or more measurements of the same sample. For example, if you measured the volume of a solution 10 times and get 10 ml each time, then your measurement method is precise. Precision can be assessed by taking multiple measurements and calculating a mean and standard deviation.

- **Accuracy** is an assessment of how close your measurement is to the actual value. For example, if you measure the volume of a 100 ml solution and get a result of 90 ml, the measurement method is not accurate. Accuracy is assessed by calibration against a known standard. So, to assess the accuracy of a balance, the mass of a reference weight of known mass would be measured.

To evaluate precision and accuracy, investigators should assess the following during both the pilot and main studies:

- the mean of replicated measurements
- the variation in these replicated measurements
- the number of samples tested
- how regularly measuring equipment requires calibration against known values.

High accuracy High precision | Low accuracy High precision | High accuracy Low precision | Low accuracy Low precision

Comparison of accuracy and precision of measurements.

RELIABILITY OF RESULTS

The natural variation in the biological material being used can be determined by measuring a sample of individuals from the population. The mean of these repeated measurements will give an indication of the true value being measured.

Experimental design should use data from the pilot study to determine the number of **replicates** required to ensure a **valid experiment** and produce **reliable results**. Good experimental design should allow for sufficient replicates and independent replicates.

- **Replicates** are multiple measurements within the same experiment; the range of values recorded is a measure of the extent of variation in the results. If there is a narrow range then the variation is low.

- **Independent replication** involves repeating the whole experiment and should be carried out to produce independent data sets. These independent data sets should be compared to determine the reliability of the results. Overall results can only be considered reliable if they can be achieved consistently.

 THINGS TO DO AND THINK ABOUT

1 Learn more about biological data distributions by researching why the distribution of weight in developed countries can no longer be thought of as normal, due to the effects of obesity.

2 Make a table to summarise the advantages and disadvantages of random, systematic and stratified sampling.

 DON'T FORGET

To avoid pseudoreplication, care should be taken, when designing an experiment that replicates are independent from each other. Pseudoreplication occurs where multiple measurements are taken from the same subject or sample, but are treated as being separate measurements when the data is analysed.

 DON'T FORGET

To determine the natural variation in a population, a determination of the type of data distribution must be made.

DON'T FORGET

Accuracy and precision are independent; a measuring method can be highly precise without being accurate, and *vice versa*.

 ONLINE

Read more about accuracy and precision at www.brightredbooks.net

DON'T FORGET

The same investigator should carry out the repeated measurements to increase reliability in a valid way.

 ONLINE

Read more about sampling at www.brightredbooks.net

PRESENTATION OF DATA

VARIATION

All biological populations show **variation**, that is, differences between individual members of a species. Variation can be either **discrete** or **continuous**. Discrete variation is where there are only a limited number of possible types of characteristic, allowing individuals to be placed into groups – examples include blood group and gender. Continuous variation describes characteristics that change gradually across a range of values, for example height and weight. Data can be qualitative, quantitative or ranked. The type of data has consequences for any graphical display or statistical tests that may be used.

Table summarising qualitative, quantitative, and ranked data.

Type of data	Explanation	Examples
Qualitative	Descriptive and difficult to measure directly. Recorded using direct counts or by observation. Difficult to analyse. Presented using a bar graph or pie chart.	Colour of leaf, softness of fur, emotions
Quantitative	Measured directly. Recorded as numbers. Easier to analyse. Presented using a line or scatter graph, or a histogram.	Concentration of solution, time, height
Ranked	Data is put into order of magnitude (from smallest to largest or least common to most common). Presented using a bar graph.	Abundance of a plant, dominance hierarchies in animals.

Biological variation tends to fall into a **normal distribution**, allowing inferences from a small sample of the population to be extended to the whole population. However, in biology, we see many other types of data distribution, such as skewed.

Normal distribution:

- Also known as a bell curve
- Most common distribution in nature
- Symmetrical
- The central value is the mean, median and mode
- For example, height of humans

Normal distribution

Skewed distribution:

- Can be negative (long tail to left) or positive (long tail to right)
- The mean is not the most common value
- The most common value (mode) is not central
- For example, the number of children in a household

Box plot

 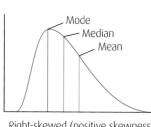

Left-skewed (negative skewness)   Right-skewed (positive skewness)

Skewed distribution

INTERPRETING DATA

In a results section, data should be presented in a clear and appropriate manner that supports data analysis and interpretation. Replicates in a study provide data that can be used to perform simple statistical calculations, such as the mean, median, mode, standard deviation and range of data, and allow the reader to determine the reliability and validity of a study.

contd

Analysing and presenting variability of data

When presenting data from experiments, it is important to use an appropriate type of graph that also shows the variability of data gathered. The **variability** of data should be shown graphically by plotting **confidence intervals** or **error bars**.

Error bars are lines through a point on a graph, parallel to an axis, which show the variation within the data. Error bars can be used to show direct measures of variation (such as the standard deviation) or probabilities (such as confidence intervals). The smaller the error bars, the less variable the data.

A **confidence interval** is a statistical estimate of the range of values within which a certain percentage of the total population would be found. For example, a 95% confidence interval shows that the range of values would include 95% of the whole population being studied.

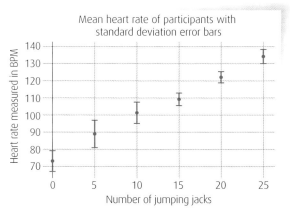

Mean heart rate of participants with standard deviation error bars

Mean temperature variation of thoroughbred horse (10-day average)

— Mean 1 horse (95% CI error bars)

Comparison of mean heart rate with standard deviation error bars

Examples of graphs with error bars displaying variation of data. Can you identify the different ways in which the confidence intervals about the mean have been represented in each case?

DON'T FORGET

Standard deviation is a statistical calculation used to quantify how much members of a group differ from the mean of the group.

ONLINE

Read more about error bars and statistical significance at www.brightredbooks.net

 THINGS TO DO AND THINK ABOUT

Line graphs are used when the independent variable is **continuous**, such as the effect of different temperatures at the rate of amylase activity.

Bar charts are used when the independent variable is discrete, such as comparing the rate of amylase activity of enzymes from different sources.

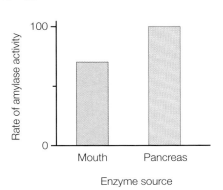

DON'T FORGET

The type of error bar (usually standard deviation or standard error) that is shown on a graph should be described on the axis label or in the graph legend.

CRITICAL EVALUATION OF BIOLOGICAL RESEARCH

EVALUATING BACKGROUND INFORMATION

An underlying principle is that background information should be clear, relevant and unambiguous. It is there to help a reader easily understand the key ideas that are relevant to the study and should not contain unnecessary or distracting information.

The background information in scientific reports should contain:

- **An explanatory title:** a title should provide a succinct explanation of the study. A good rule of thumb is that it should mention the biologically relevant independent and dependent variables, as well as the study organism and context.

- **A summary or abstract:** this should provide more information than the title but still be a short statement. It must include an outline of both the aims and the findings. It is easy to forget to include a summary of the findings but it is important in science communication to get these across as quickly as possible in the report.

- **An introduction:** this should explain the purpose and context of study, including the use of several sources, supporting statements, citations and references. The introduction should provide any information required by the reader to understand the aims, hypotheses, methods, results and discussion. An introduction should explain why the study has been carried out and place the study in the context of existing understanding. Key points should be summarised and supporting and contradictory information identified. Decisions regarding basic selection of study methods and organisms should be covered, as should the aims and hypotheses.

- **A method:** this section should contain sufficient information to allow another investigator to repeat the work.

EVALUATING EXPERIMENTAL DESIGN

The validity and reliability of the experimental design should be evaluated. It is essential that the selected experimental design should test the intended aim or hypothesis. An experimental design that does not test the intended aim or hypothesis is invalid. Not every experimental design manages to be both valid and reliable, so it is worth looking out for the following:

- **Does the design allow treatment effects to be identified in a valid way?** Treatment effects should be compared to controls and any confounding variables. The validity of an experiment may be compromised where factors other than the independent variable influence the value of the dependent variable.

- **Is the data representative and unbiased?** Selection bias may have prevented a representative sample being selected. Selection bias may mask or falsify a treatment effect. Sample size may not be sufficient to decide without bias whether the modification to the independent variable has caused an effect in the dependent variable.

EVALUATING DATA ANALYSIS

Always check that the use of graphs, mean, median, mode, standard deviation and range in interpreting data is appropriate.

Confidence intervals or error bars should be used to indicate the variability of data around a mean.

If the treatment average differs from the control average sufficiently for their confidence intervals not to overlap then the data can be said to be different.

A statistically significant result is one that is unlikely to be due to chance alone.

In results, data should be presented in a clear, logical manner suitable for analysis. Data may be quantitative or qualitative, depending on the variables investigated.

EVALUATING CONCLUSIONS

Conclusions should always refer to the aim, the results and the hypothesis, and the validity and reliability of the experimental design should be taken into account.

Consideration should be given as to whether the results can be attributed to correlation or causation.

Correlation exists if there is a relationship between two variables. Evaluating the strength of **correlations** between two variables can be achieved by examining the data and by considering how closely the two variables respond to each other. Strong correlations often show a linear relationship, the strength of which can be shown by carrying out a regression analysis. The strength of the correlation is judged by the closeness of the individual data points to the line of best fit.

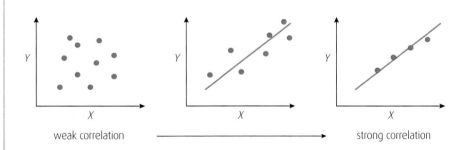

weak correlation ⟶ strong correlation

ONLINE

Read more about correlation at www.brightredbooks.net

Demonstrating **causation** is more difficult as correlation does not imply causation. Causation can only be shown where all confounding variables are adequately controlled and so is difficult to demonstrate in observational studies. A well-designed experimental study may allow conclusions to be drawn about causation. Causation exists if the changes in the values of the independent variable are known to cause changes to the value of the dependent variable.

Conclusions should also refer to existing knowledge and the results of other investigations. Scientific writing should reveal an awareness of the contribution of scientific research to increasing scientific knowledge and to the social, economic and industrial life of the community.

 THINGS TO DO AND THINK ABOUT

A positive correlation exists when an increase in one variable is accompanied by an increase in the other variable. A negative correlation exists when an increase in one variable is accompanied by a decrease in the other variable.

YOUR PROJECT

CHOOSING A TOPIC

The project provides opportunities for you to put into practice your investigative skills, honed during the taught unit. It must be a piece of **individual work**, so group work and joint project are not permitted.

Your teacher/lecturer will help you to choose a suitable topic that interests you. It could be something that you have covered in the AH Biology course, though it doesn't have to be; there may be something that you learnt in Higher or found out about from another source that leads you to a suitable topic for a project. Useful sources for initial reading include school and undergraduate textbooks, newspaper and media items, medical and government reports, websites and scientific journals such as *School Science Review*, *New Scientist* and *Scientific American*.

A suitable topic

You may have a great idea for a project topic, but it needs to be suitable to your situation. What does this mean?

- Obviously your project has to be on a **biological topic** and it must be at a level appropriate to the **demands** of Advanced Higher Biology.

- It must include **experimental or survey work** and can't be purely a technical exercise in statistics or computing. (And if you are doing AH Chemistry or AH Geography, for example, the topics of your investigations need to be different.)

- Do not be over-ambitious. Your investigation is unlikely to be a piece of original research, but it will be **new to you**. A **simple project**, able to be completed in the time available, is likely to be the most successful.

A practicable topic

During discussions with your teacher/lecturer, consider the **time and the resources** available to you to gather sufficient data (including the replicates or sample size).

Biological context	Independent variable	Dependent variable
What is it that you plan to investigate?	What will you change in the biological system?	What will you look for as your result?
For example, an enzyme, tissue, organism, habitat, etc.	How will you change the conditions?	How will you measure the result?

Limitations might include: equipment, biological materials, chemicals, safety, laboratory facilities, season of year.

You need to think about the **aim of the project** and how you will gather results. The aim has three parts and they all need to be practicable for your investigation to be feasible.

Making a timeline

When you have sorted out what experimental or survey work you will do to investigate your topic, you need to make a realistic timeline of the work that you plan. You will need a good level of **self-motivation and organisation** so that you can stick to the timeline. You may have to be flexible – your plans may have to change as your work progresses. Making an early and committed start to the work will allow time for this flexibility; if you start late, the final report deadline may catch up with you.

KEEPING A RECORD

Keeping a regular, clear and accurate record of your project work is crucial to producing a good report. You should also record your results and other data in a way that makes it easy for you to follow and understand. It is much easier later if you note the **date of each entry** in your record!

contd

Your record should include:

- short notes on the ideas you have in the early stages of planning your project (including ideas you might later dismiss)
- a brief record of the discussions you have with your teacher/lecturer and other scientists (including any decisions that you make)
- notes from your background biology research into the topic of the project (including reference details)
- a record of experimental methods and procedures, results obtained and an analysis of your results (using calculations, tables, graphs, diagrams or photographs as appropriate). This would include any preliminary work carried out as a pilot study (e.g. developing techniques or apparatus; devising observational, experimental or sampling procedures).

Periodically, your teacher/lecturer will check on how you are progressing in your project and they will want to see your record. These checks will happen regularly to ensure that procedures, safety, resources and timescales are still appropriate. Although you are expected to work autonomously, your teacher/lecturer will provide advice and support and, if these discussions lead to a change in your plan, it is important that you keep a note of the reasons for any changes.

THE PILOT STUDY

To pass the Investigative Biology area of study in full, you are required to plan and carry out a pilot study for your project, as well as to pass the written test. This pilot study could be assessed from the notes in your project record or as a separate written report. (If you have already passed the knowledge assessments for the other two areas of study, passing the pilot study will also allow you to pass these areas of study in full.)

The table below shows what you need to do to pass the pilot study.

Checkpoint	Suggestions on how to achieve the checkpoint
1. State the aim of the project and formulate questions or hypotheses to be investigated	Develop ideas for your project by reviewing and discussing previous learning and/or researching appropriate sources of information. The purpose of your project must be clear and you must formulate questions to be investigated and/or hypotheses to be tested.
2. Devise appropriate experimental, observational and sampling procedures, techniques and apparatus	The procedures you devise must be appropriate to the aim of the project. You must select an appropriate procedure after considering or trying alternatives or becoming proficient in the procedure.
3. Consider the need for controls and replicate treatments or samples	You must consider the use of negative and positive controls and the control of potential confounding variables as appropriate. The need for repeat measurements, replicate treatments or samples and independently replicated experiments must be considered.
4. Take into account the ethical use of living materials, human subjects and the conservation of natural habitats	Take into account any ethical issues relevant to the project.
5. Identify potential hazards, assess their associated risks and apply appropriate control measures	Be aware of any potential hazards and use the appropriate control measures to control risks in carrying out the Investigation.
6. Make observations and record measurements with appropriate precision and accuracy	Record your observations and/or measurements in a planned and organised way. Consider the precision and accuracy of your results.
7. Use initial results to devise further experiments or to confirm the appropriateness of a procedure for further work	Review experimental findings and identify if further steps are needed.

THE PROJECT REPORT

The final report is sent to the SQA. It has to be written up in a formal style and is worth 25% of your total marks. The latest guidance on how to present the report (along with the detailed marking scheme) is found at **Coursework Information** on the SQA AH Biology website.

WRITING THE REPORT

MAKE SURE YOU FOLLOW THE INSTRUCTIONS

The Project Report submitted to SQA is worth 25% of the final Advanced Higher mark. It is worth ensuring that your report matches the examination requirements as closely as possible; double check using the **Coursework Information** on the SQA AH Biology website.

An investigation report should be structured logically and written clearly. The main body of the text should be around 3000 to 3600 words.

Remember that an examiner will have to mark your work, so make it as **logical** and as easy to read as possible. Communicate **clearly** and honestly, and with enough **detail** so that your investigation could be repeated by anyone who has read your report.

Make sure that all your **raw data** is included; if there is a lot of data, include it as an appendix. The rest of this section offers advice in areas where candidates frequently and unnecessarily lose marks.

The report must include the following sections:

- Title page
- Contents page
- Abstract
- Introduction
- Procedures
- Results
- Discussion
- Reference list.

The detailed marking scheme for the Project Report and guidance on what to write for each section of the Project report can be is found at **Coursework Information** on the SQA AH Biology website; the link can be found at www.brightredbooks.net

YOUR INTRODUCTION

Your introduction must include a clear statement of the aims of the Project (despite the fact that you have already stated these in the abstract), along with relevant hypotheses or questions.

In this section, you must also include an account of the relevant background theory at a level appropriate to Advanced Higher. You are expected to provide plenty of detail. Remember, the examiner may know little about your chosen topic, so your introduction should provide the background information. You must also justify the biological importance of the Project. Why did you think it was worth doing in terms of biological knowledge? Does the topic have wider implications?

GRAPHICAL PRESENTATION

It is essential to summarise your results using appropriate graphs. But graphs should not appear alone; every graph that you draw should be accompanied by a table showing the relevant processed data.

You may be adept at using electronic software to manipulate the axes of graphs to suit your data, so that the results are presented in a correct scientific manner. If you are at all unsure, you are advised to draw your graphs by hand. Check your graphs to make sure they present your data clearly:

contd

- Are the axes labelled, including units?

- Does each axis have a value marked at its start? This is often a zero but it can be a different value if the data range is not close to zero. For example, heart rate data might be on a scale from 60 to 140 beats per minute.

- Are the scales evenly spaced?

- Have you used line graphs for continuous variables and bar graphs/pie charts for discontinuous variables?

- Have you presented your data sets so that they can be compared easily?

DON'T FORGET

You could use the styles of referencing below for Advanced Higher Biology.

YOUR CONCLUSIONS AND EVALUATION

The discussion section is the most important part of the Project Report. You must refer back to what you have written earlier in the report and discuss your findings in a critical and scientific manner.

In your discussion section, you need to provide a clear statement of the **overall conclusion**, stating how your results relate to the biological effect you were investigating. Your conclusion must relate to the aim of the project and be valid for the results obtained. Do not be tempted to over-interpret what you have found!

Essentially, this section is your chance to explain whether your independent variable has influenced your dependent variable. In order to do this well, you should describe how your **procedures** were robust enough for you to be able to detect an effect. You should give clear descriptions of the features of your good experimental design that contributed to accuracy, reliability and validity. You must also explain very carefully how confident you can be about your **results**. Your discussion should cover the degree of **variation** in your results **within samples**, **between treatments** and, finally, **between replicates**.

REFERENCES

A **reference** is any piece of material to which a writer 'refers' in the text. You can either use the **Harvard system** or the **Vancouver system** in your Project Report.

The Harvard system uses bracketed citations with the name(s) of the author(s) and the year of publication. These direct the reader to the reference list which has the references in alphabetical order. For example, the authors of this book (Lloyd and Morgan, 2019) find that they often refer to Raven and Johnson (2002) and Begon *et al.* (2006) when planning their teaching. The journal *Biological Sciences Review* is also recommended as it contains many articles relevant to Advanced Higher Biology, such as one on growing algae for food (Roberts, 2007). You can also use reliable websites and reference them in the same way; so we have used the Project Assessment Task document to help us write this page (SQA, 2019).

The Vancouver system shows citations by using numbers, either in brackets or as superscripts. These direct the reader to the reference list which has the references in their numerical order. For example, the authors of this book (1) find that they often refer to Raven and Johnson (2) and Begon *et al.* (3) when planning their teaching. The journal *Biological Sciences Review* is also recommended as it contains many articles relevant to Advanced Higher Biology, such as one on growing algae for food (4). You can also use reliable websites and reference them in the same way; so we have used the Project Assessment Task document to help us write this page (5).

Example: Harvard Reference list

Begon, M., Townsend, C.R. & Harper, J.L. (2006) *Ecology: From Individuals to Ecosystems (4th Edition)*, Blackwell Publishing, Oxford
Lloyd, D. & Morgan, G. (2019) *Advanced Higher Biology*, Bright Red Publishing, Edinburgh
Raven, P.H. & Johnson, G.B. (2002) *Biology (6th Edition)*, McGraw-Hill, New York
Roberts, D. (2007) Aquaculture *Biological Science Review* Vol. **20** (No. 1), pages 2–6
SQA (2019) *Advanced Higher Biology Project Assessment Task*. Available from: https://www.sqa.org.uk/files_ccc/ GAInfoAHBiology.pdf [Visited: July 2019]

Example: Vancouver Reference list

Lloyd, D. & Morgan, G. (2019) *Advanced Higher Biology*, Bright Red Publishing, Edinburgh
Raven, P.H. & Johnson, G.B. (2002) *Biology (6th Edition)*, McGraw-Hill, New York
Begon, M., Townsend, C.R. & Harper, J.L. *(2006) Ecology: From Individuals to Ecosystems (4th Edition)*, Blackwell Publishing, Oxford
Roberts, D. (2007) Aquaculture *Biological Science Review* Vol. **20** (No. 1), pages 2–6
SQA (2019) *Advanced Higher Biology Project Assessment Task*. Available from: https://www.sqa.org.uk/files_ccc/ GAInfoAHBiology.pdf [Visited: July 2019]